DISCOVERY GUIDE

FAITH LESSONS™
in the dust
of the rabbi

BECOMING A DISCIPLE

FOCUS ON THE FAMILY®

Ray Vander Laan
with Stephen & Amanda Sorenson

ZONDERVAN

ZONDERVAN.com/
AUTHORTRACKER
follow your favorite authors

In the Dust of the Rabbi Small Group Edition Discovery Guide
Copyright © 2006 by Ray Vander Laan

Requests for information should be addressed to:

Zondervan, Grand Rapids, Michigan 49530

ISBN-10: 0-310-27120-7
ISBN-13: 978-0-310-27120-8

Interior design by Michelle Espinoza

Printed in the United States of America

08 09 10 11 12 • 18 17 16 15 14 13 12 11 10 9 8 7

contents

introduction

Because God speaks to us through the Scriptures, studying them is a rewarding experience. The inspired human authors of the Bible, as well as those to whom the words were originally given, were primarily Jews living in the Near East. God's words and actions spoke to them with such power, clarity, and purpose that they wrote them down and carefully preserved them as an authoritative body of literature.

God's use of human servants in revealing himself resulted in writings that clearly bear the stamp of time and place. The message of the Scriptures is, of course, eternal and unchanging—but the circumstances and conditions of the people of the Bible are unique to their times. Consequently, we most clearly understand God's truth when we know the cultural context within which he spoke and acted, and the perception of the people with whom he communicated. This does not mean that God's revelation is unclear if we don't know the cultural context. Rather, by learning how to think and approach life as the people of the Bible did, modern Christians will deepen their appreciation and understanding of God's Word. To fully apply the message of the Bible, we must enter their world and familiarize ourselves with their culture.

That is the purpose of this study. The events and people of the Bible are presented in their original settings. Although the DVD segments offer the latest archaeological research, this series is not intended to be a definitive historical, cultural, or geographical study of the lands and times of the Bible. No original scientific discoveries are revealed here. My goal is simply to help us better understand God's revealed mission for our lives by enabling us to hear and see his words in their original context.

go! And make Disciples

The mission of God's people has always been to live *so that the world would know that their God was the true God.* This was true when the Hebrews left Egypt and possessed the Promised Land. This was true during the years of the exile in Babylon. It was true during the time Jesus lived on earth after the Jews had returned to Israel. And it was true for the disciples of Jesus who followed him as their Rabbi and, after his death and resurrection, obeyed his command to go out into the world and make disciples.

When Jesus came to earth to bring the good news of the kingdom of God and to offer himself as the perfect sacrifice to redeem the whole human race, he also chose disciples who would continue proclaiming his message and making disciples long after he returned to heaven. Jesus selected his disciples from a unique people in a unique place—a four-by-six-mile area on the northwestern shores of the Sea of Galilee. The Jews living in this part of Israel were the most obedient, faithful followers of God to be found. These people knew the Scriptures, they knew how to apply the teaching of Scripture, and they were committed to obeying God in everything every day of their lives. From among them, Jesus chose a handful to carry the news of his kingdom to the world.

To some, Jesus' disciples would seem like an unlikely group. To their world, they weren't the brightest and the best Bible scholars; most of them were fishermen. They didn't know their way around the huge, sophisticated cities of the Roman Empire; they came from small, rural villages. But they had just what Jesus needed—the commitment, the passion, the desire to be his *talmidim*. For three and a half years, the disciples walked with Jesus. They followed him everywhere. They did everything they could to learn to be like Jesus—to know and interpret the Scriptures as he did, to pray as he did, to obey God's laws as he did, to love as he did, to proclaim the news of God's kingdom as he did, and to make disciples as he did.

Before he ascended to heaven, Jesus commanded them to go out into the world and make disciples. And they did. One of the places they went was Asia Minor—the most sophisticated, prosperous, immoral, perverted, educated, and religious (but pagan) region in the whole Roman Empire! And when the disciples lived out the message of the kingdom of God and made disciples in Asia Minor, it impacted that region like an earthquake. In little more than a century, that region had become predominantly Christian.

In this study, we will investigate the world they went into and how the disciples made such a great impact. This is important to us because our world is much like the world of Asia Minor. If we expect to make the impact the disciples did, then we must learn to be like them—that is, like Jesus. The life of faith is not a vague, otherworldly experience. Rather, it is being faithful to God right now, in the place and time in which he has put us. God wants his people in the game, not on the bench. Our mission as Christians today is the same one God gave to the Israelites when they possessed the Promised Land, the same one Jesus gave to his disciples. We are to love the Lord our God with all our heart, with all our soul, and with all our might, and to love our neighbors as ourselves so that through us *the world may know that our God is the one true God.*

The Assumptions of Biblical Writers

Biblical writers assumed that their readers were familiar with Near Eastern geography, history, and culture. They used a language, which like all languages, is bound by culture and time. Therefore, understanding the Scriptures involves more than knowing what the words mean. We need to understand those words from the perspective of the people who used them.

Unfortunately, many Christians do not have even a basic knowledge of the world and people of the Bible. This series is designed to help solve that problem. We will be studying the people and events of the Bible in their geographical, historical, and cultural contexts. Once we know the *who, what,* and *where* of a Bible story, we will be able to better understand the *why.* By deepening our understanding of God's Word, we can strengthen our relationship with God.

The people whom God chose as his instruments—the people to whom he revealed himself—lived in the Near East where people typically described their world and themselves in concrete terms. Their language was one of pictures, metaphors, and examples rather than ideas, definitions, and abstractions. Whereas we might describe God as omniscient or onmipresent (knowing everything and present everywhere), they would have preferred to describe God by saying, "The Lord is my

Shepherd." Thus, the Bible is filled with concrete images: God is our Father, and we are his children. God is the Potter, and we are the clay. Jesus is the Lamb killed on Passover. The kingdom of heaven is like the yeast a woman took and mixed into flour. He will separate the people as a shepherd separates the sheep from the goats.

These people had an Eastern mind-set rather than a Western mind-set. Whereas Westerners tend to collect information to find the right answer, Hebrew thought stresses the process of discovery as well as the answer. So as you go through this study, use it as an opportunity to deepen your understanding of who God is and to grow in your relationship with him.

when the rabbi says "come"

Discipleship was at the heart of Jesus' ministry, so it's not surprising that the word *disciple* is used more than 250 times in the New Testament. In fact, the New Testament is the story of disciples written by disciples who wanted to make disciples. And those disciples dramatically changed their world!

But is the disciple-making mission of Jesus and his followers as clear, compelling, and effective nearly two thousand years later? Not really. Discipleship as Jesus and his followers knew it is not part of Western Christian culture today. Contemporary Christianity does not always make discipleship central to the faith. Many who call themselves Christians don't even know what a disciple is. While we readily agree that it is essential to believe in Jesus as our Savior, we tend to treat his lordship in our lives as a desirable option, like the color we choose when we buy a new car — nice, but not essential. If we don't recognize the importance of discipleship, we tend to think that obeying God's commands is a worthwhile goal but is less important than "being saved." We view discipleship as a goal that only a few "all-star" believers can attain.

Jesus and his disciples had a very different view of discipleship. They made no distinction between "being saved" and living in obedience to God. To be saved was to be totally committed to a life of obedience — to walk as the Rabbi walked, to become like him. They did not do this in order to *be* saved, but rather because they *were* saved. Thus the goal of the community of Jesus is not to make *converts* but to make *disciples*. Salvation, of course, is essential, but it is the entrance to the path of discipleship rather than the final destination. That is why the apostle James wrote, "Faith by itself, if it is not accompanied by action, is dead" (James 2:17).

In this session, we will consider what Jesus means by his call, "Come, follow me." His is a call to radical discipleship, a concept Dallas Willard captures well:

> When Jesus walked among humankind, there was a certain simplicity to being a disciple. Primarily it meant to go with him, in an attitude of study, obedience, and imitation. There were no correspondence courses. One knew what to do and what it would cost.... Family and friends were deserted for long periods to go with Jesus as he walked from place to place announcing, showing, and explaining the governance of God. Disciples had to be with him to learn what he did.[1]

Just as God miraculously blessed the early disciples' desire and commitment to become more like Jesus the Rabbi, God desires the same of us. He calls us to reclaim the ancient practice of discipleship that was central to Jesus' life and message. So let's walk in the footsteps of ancient disciples for a while. Let's explore the communities and culture in which they lived. Let's examine the practices of first-century rabbis and their disciples—their love for and knowledge of Scripture and their passionate desire to give up everything in order to obey God as their rabbi did. As we discover the world in which discipleship was born and practiced, we will better understand Jesus' call to be his disciples.

opening Thoughts (4 minutes)

The Very Words of God

> *We know that we have come to know him if we obey his commands. The man who says, "I know him," but does not do what he commands is a liar, and the truth is not in him. But if anyone obeys his word, God's love is truly made complete in him. This is how we know we are in him: Whoever claims to live in him must walk as Jesus did.*
>
> 1 John 2:3–6

Think About It

When it came time to choose his disciples and launch his ministry, Jesus did not go to Jerusalem — the first place *we* might have gone — but to the sparsely populated hills surrounding the Sea of Galilee. Why? What was it about Galilee that captured his attention above all other places in Israel?

DVD Notes (≥8 minutes)

Scythopolis and Bethsaida: cities in contrast

Galilee, where discipleship flourished

The building blocks of discipleship

Becoming a disciple

DVD Highlights (4 minutes)

1. What was unique about the Jews who lived in Galilee?

   In what ways did the things they were passionate about differ from the driving passions of people who lived in Scythopolis (Beth Shean)?

2. What impact do you think the Galileans' understanding of community had on the ways they practiced their faith in everyday life?

3. What was the central focus of worship in the synagogues of Galilee in Jesus' day?

   What effect did their love for the words of God have on daily life in Galilee?

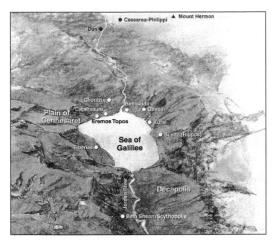

Sea of Galilee cities

small group bible discovery and discussion (14 minutes)

The Building Blocks of Discipleship

When Christians today talk about being a *disciple*, we don't mean exactly the same thing as the Galileans of Jesus' day. Discipleship was a core value in Galilean society. In fact, Galilee was where the world came to become disciples of the great rabbis. So let's open our Bibles and open our eyes to discover what discipleship meant in the world of Jesus.

1. What is a disciple? (See Matthew 4:18–22; 10:24–25; John 8:31; 1 Corinthians 11:1; 1 John 2:3–6.)

Think About It

Discipleship begins with belief, but that is only the beginning. A disciple obeys the Rabbi's teaching. A Christian disciple not only believes Jesus is the Messiah but also is passionately devoted to doing what the Rabbi (Jesus) commands.

Ray Vander Laan

---

2. What do the following verses reveal about the three building blocks of discipleship—obedience, community, the Word of God? (See Deuteronomy 6:4–7; Matthew 5:17–19; 9:35–36; Acts 16:15; Ephesians 2:19–22.)

3. When large crowds began following Jesus, he spoke to them about what it meant to be his disciple. How did he describe discipleship, and why do you think he said these things? (See Luke 14:27–33.)

Understanding the Language of Discipleship

If we are to understand what discipleship meant to Jesus and his disciples, we need insight into the biblical meaning and usage of several words:

Talmid (*Talmidim*, pl.) is the Hebrew word for *disciple*. The *talmid* willingly left home, family, and occupation to be with the rabbi because he wanted more than anything else in the world to be like the rabbi (teacher) in his walk with God. As the rabbi lived and taught his understanding of the Scripture, his *talmid* listened to him, watched him, followed him, memorized his words, and imitated his walk with God. Eventually the *talmid* became a teacher who had his own disciples who wanted to learn from him how to walk with God.

Haver (*Haverim*, pl.) is the Hebrew root word that refers to deep social bonds between people. It is translated as "friend" but means much more. It denotes a relationship that is stronger than death itself. It can be used in reference to a close-knit group of people, or to disciples and their rabbi who are deeply committed to each other and to their common goals (as in John 15:12–16).

Mathetes, the Greek word translated "disciple," refers to *talmid* as well as to individuals who are interested but who have not renounced everything to follow the rabbi.

4. Why do you think Jesus chose disciples from small, rural, seemingly unimportant villages to take his message to the sophisticated culture of the Roman world? What did they have to offer people in a world of success, personal comfort, beautiful temples, exciting arenas, vast libraries, magnificent theaters, and stimulating gymnasia?

5. In what ways do our lifestyle choices and our culture undermine a total commitment to discipleship? What do you think we can do to reclaim our passion for God? A faith community? Obedience? The Scriptures?

Shocking Contrasts

Startling contrasts existed between the extravagant buildings of the sprawling Greek and Roman cities and the plain, utilitarian communities of Galilee.

Galilee was largely rural and agricultural. The only public buildings in Galilee—synagogues—were used as community centers, schools, and places of worship. Village streets were usually unpaved, and people carried water to their homes from nearby springs and wells. Most Galileans worked hard, but they were not poor. They knew the Scriptures well, were very religious, and avoided pagan practices.

The ruins of the city of Beth Shean (left) in contrast to the ruins of the village of Bethsaida.

Inhabitants of nearby Roman cities, on the other hand, could enjoy every known luxury and pleasure. Those who could afford it lived in elaborate villas with running water. Streets were paved with stones and equipped with sewers. Goods from every corner of the empire could be bought in the agoras (markets), and an array of gods could be worshiped in pagan temples. The people could train their bodies and minds in gymnasiums and libraries and could amuse themselves in the baths, brothels, theaters, and arenas.

Yet by 200 AD, the huge area of Asia Minor had a significant Christian population because God used ordinary Galileans to share the good news of the kingdom of heaven!

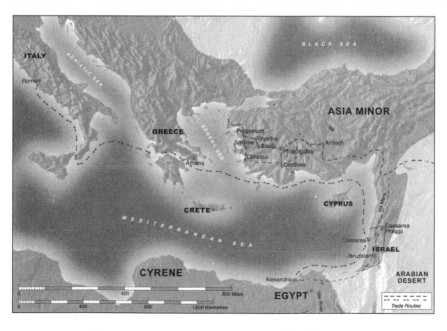

Asia Minor and the Roman Empire. In comparison to Galilee — even all of Israel — Asia Minor was huge! Yet Jesus' disciples took the message of the kingdom of heaven to many of the large, sophisticated, pagan cities situated along the busy trade routes that passed through Asia Minor. The main trade route, the Via Maris, passed through Galilee connecting Egypt to the heart of the ancient world.

ꜰaith Lesson (4 minutes)

When talking about the people of Bethsaida, Ray said, "We tend to think of ourselves as individuals. In their world, they … understood that community is more important than the individual."

1. What role does community play in your walk with Jesus?

2. In what way(s) might your individualism affect your view of discipleship—and your commitment to be a disciple of Jesus?

3. Which aspects of spiritual community in Chorazin might you want to incorporate into your life?

closing (1 minute)

Read 1 John 2:6 aloud: "Whoever claims to live in him must walk as Jesus did."

Then ask God to use this session and your time of personal study to help you see discipleship as Jesus sees it. Ask him to give you a heart that desires above all else to walk in the dust of the Rabbi.

Memorize

Whoever claims to live in him must walk as Jesus did.

1 John 2:6

walking with the rabbi day by day

In-Depth Personal Study Sessions

Day one/Galilee:
The Heart of Jesus' Ministry

The Very Words of God

Jesus went throughout Galilee, teaching in their synagogues, preaching the good news of the kingdom, and healing every disease and sickness among the people.

Matthew 4:23

Bible Discovery

Why Galilee?

Although Jesus traveled through much of Israel from Phoenicia to Jerusalem, he focused his ministry in the small area of Galilee. Here, within about a four-by-six-mile area on the north and northwestern shores of the Sea of Galilee, he lived and taught in places named Bethsaida, Capernaum, Chorazin, Magdala, and Gennesareth.

1. Why did Jesus choose Galilee as the focal point of his ministry, and what was his message? (See Matthew 4:12–17.)

2. Who was the audience Jesus wanted to reach with his message, and how serious was he about delivering it? (See Matthew 10:5 – 7; 15:21 – 28.)

3. Like any rabbi, Jesus taught using metaphors and images familiar to his audience. (See Matthew 7:15 – 20; 13:47 – 52; Luke 20:9 – 19.) What do these passages reveal about the life and people of Galilee? How do you know the people understood what Jesus said?

4. How did Jesus respond when his message of repentance and preparation for the kingdom of heaven moved people to action? How did he respond when it did *not* seem to have an impact? (See Matthew 11:20 – 24; 15:21 – 28; Mark 2:1 – 12.)

Worth Observing ...

For the first fifty to seventy-five years after Jesus ascended to heaven, the Christian community was stronger in Galilee than anywhere else in the world. Perhaps the people of Chorazin, Bethsaida, and Capernaum took Jesus' rebuke to heart (Matthew 11:20 – 24).

Reflection

No matter where he went, people paid attention to Jesus. Whether they wanted to or not, it seems they recognized in him the authority and presence of the kingdom of God.

> What have you learned about Jesus and his message through his ministry in Galilee?

> What about his message has caught your attention? What is your response?

Day Two/what is a Rabbi?

The Very Words of God

Now there was a man of the Pharisees named Nicodemus, a member of the Jewish ruling council. He came to Jesus at night and said, "Rabbi, we know you are a teacher who has come from God."

John 3:1–2

Bible Discovery

The Role of the Rabbi

In Jesus' day, becoming like the rabbi was the driving motivation of a disciple's life! For years a disciple wanted to hear everything the rabbi said, know everything the rabbi knew, and do everything the rabbi did. Today, however, the idea of respecting someone so much that we would dedicate great effort to following him so closely is foreign to us. What was so special about a rabbi?

Profile of a Rabbi

In Jesus' day, a rabbi was not the formal head of a religious community or synagogue as we think of a rabbi today. Instead, *rabbi* was an honored term of respect given to one who interpreted and taught the Hebrew Bible. *Rabbi* meant "my superior" or "my master" and came from a Hebrew root meaning "great" or "many." Disciples and others used this term to refer to great scholars and teachers of the Scriptures who were also known as "sages." After the destruction of the temple in Jerusalem in AD 70, *rabbi* became a formal title for sage.

Rabbis played an important role in the Jewish spiritual culture because there were no formal seminaries at the time of Jesus. Each rabbi taught his disciples how the Torah should be interpreted and obeyed, and his disciples willingly submitted to that interpretation. A rabbi, then, was an honored teacher who was well versed in the text of the Hebrew Bible. He was highly respected for his knowledge, interpretation, and teaching of Scripture as well as for his personal righteousness. Following a rabbi required a deep commitment on the part of the disciple who would live with and follow the rabbi day in and day out for years in order to learn to be like him and live in obedience to God as the rabbi did.

For the Galileans, walking with God took priority over everything. So a rabbi and his disciples typically were highly

---

respected by others in the community. A family or extended family group usually provided housing and food for a rabbi and his disciples. Because of the high respect for study of the Torah, and the fact that the rabbi was leading other people to the kingdom of heaven and the life to come, each disciple was expected to honor the rabbi even more than his own father. It is difficult for Christians today to imagine such love and commitment to a human teacher, but that was the norm in Galilee.

1. A first-century rabbi had a unique lifestyle, and the Scriptures give us insight into what his daily life was like.

   a. Where did a rabbi live? How did he find food and shelter? (See Luke 7:36; 8:1 – 3; 10:5 – 11.)

   b. Where did a rabbi teach, and who listened to him? (See Matthew 5:1 – 2; Mark 6:6; Luke 4:14 – 16; 7:36, 40 – 43.)

2. What teaching technique common to the Galilean rabbis did Jesus use? How did the way Jesus taught his disciples differ from how he taught the crowds? (See Mark 4:33 – 34.)

3. What types of people recognized Jesus as a rabbi (teacher)? What does this tell you about his teaching? (See Luke 7:39–40; 12:13; 19:39; 20:27–28, 39–40; John 1:35–38.)

Did You Know?

All teaching by the early rabbis attempted to explain, interpret, and apply some portion of the Hebrew Bible. To the audience, the validity of the teaching depended on the rabbi's ability to use a variety of passages in new and creative ways, to illustrate the teaching with parable or metaphor, and to ground the teaching in text. Whether they wanted to or not, people who heard Jesus teach recognized that he taught with authority. (See Matthew 7:28–29; 21:23–27; Mark 1:27–28.)

In fact, Jesus best fit the type of rabbi believed to have s'mikhah, the authority to make new interpretations of the Torah. Most teachers of the law could only teach accepted interpretations. Teachers with authority, however, could make new interpretations and pass legal judgments.

Reflection

In Matthew 10:1–14, we read the instructions Jesus gave to his disciples when he sent them out. This passage gives us a picture of what everyday life was like for his disciples. It shows us how Jesus expected them to live and what he expected them to do. Read this passage and consider how committed you are to Jesus, your Rabbi.

Fact File
Educated as a Rabbi

The Mishnah[2] describes the educational process for a young Jewish boy during Jesus' time:

> At five years old [one is fit] for the Scripture, at ten years the Mishnah [oral Torah interpretations], at thirteen for [the fulfilling of] the commandments, at fifteen the Talmud [making rabbinic interpretations], at eighteen the bride-chamber, at twenty pursuing a vocation, at thirty for authority [able to teach others].

This passage clearly describes the education of an exceptional student, because few students became teachers. It also indicates the centrality of the Hebrew text in the education of Jews in Galilee. A comparison of this description to Jesus' life shows that he closely followed the customs of his time and place:

- Jesus "grew in wisdom" as a boy (Luke 2:52).
- Jesus reached the "fulfilling of the commandments" indicated by his first Passover at age twelve (Luke 2:41–47). His excellent questions for teachers in the temple during that Passover indicate the study he had done.
- Jesus learned a trade with his father (Matthew 13:55).
- Jesus spent time with John the Baptist, a rabbi (John 3:22–26; 4:1–3). The fact that Jesus and his disciples were baptizing might suggest that Jesus and John may have studied together or with the same teacher. No teacher is mentioned in Scripture, although Jesus did say he "learned" (John 15:15).
- Jesus became a rabbi at "about thirty" (Luke 3:23).

day three/know, love, and obey the text

The Very Words of God

Blessed rather are those who hear the word of God and obey it.

Luke 11:28

Bible Discovery

Living by the Word

Jesus came to people who knew the Scriptures. They expended great effort to study and memorize the text, to debate its meaning, to teach it to other people, and—above all else—to obey it. As you take a closer look at Jesus' ministry, consider how essential the text was to all that he did and said.

1. Read the following passages and note Jesus' love for the Scriptures, his desire to learn and understand them, his faithfulness in obeying them, and his commitment to teaching them to others. How badly do you want to follow his example?

   a. Matthew 4:1–11

   b. Luke 2:41–47, 52

   c. John 15:14–15

Did You Know?

For the Jews in Galilee, knowing and obeying the Scriptures was as essential to life as food and water. They memorized significant portions of Scripture in synagogue schools. They heard it read aloud during synagogue prayers and when the rabbis read and discussed it. After all, how could one rightly interpret and obey God's commands without knowing the text? How could one walk with God without knowing what he said? Not to know the text was unthinkable.

2. When he taught, Jesus continually referred to the Hebrew Bible that was so familiar to his audience. In the book of Matthew alone, he quoted the Hebrew text at least thirty-eight times! As you read the following passages, notice how easily the text flowed from his lips as he spoke. Why did he base so much of his teaching on the Hebrew Scriptures? Could Jesus have shared the Scriptures effectively if he had not memorized them? Why or why not? (See Matthew 5:21, 27, 31, 33, 38, 43; 9:10–13; 12:1–8.)

3. What do the following passages show you about Jesus' knowledge of Scripture and his commitment to obey it? (See Matthew 4:13–17; 8:16–17; 21:1–6; 26:52–56.)

For Greater Understanding …

In Matthew 5:17, Jesus said, "Do not think that I have come to abolish the Law or the Prophets; I have not come to abolish them but to fulfill them." In this statement, Jesus used technical rabbinic terminology. *Abolish* meant to interpret Scripture so that it would not be obeyed as God desired. *Fulfill* meant to interpret Scripture so it would be obeyed as God intended. So when Jesus used these terms, his audience would have heard him say, "I did not come to misinterpret the Scripture so you would not keep it correctly. I came to interpret it so that you will know how to keep it correctly."

---

4. In what way did Jesus use his knowledge of the Scriptures in Luke 24:13 – 32? Which Scripture did Jesus use? What do you think his teaching must have meant to the two men when they realized who he was?

Reflection

Jesus came from a community that knew the Scriptures, and he expected his disciples to follow his example and become like him. He expects no less from his followers today. Yet many of us do not know much about the text he knew and loved, and we have memorized even less of it.

How can we do what Jesus commands if we do not know his Word?

Is it time to dedicate yourself to knowing your Bible and using it as the foundation for your life and witness? How will you begin?

How would memorizing Scripture reinforce your desire to live by its truth in your daily life?

If you are serious about being a disciple, ask God to fill you with his Spirit and give you a desire to become more like Jesus who knew and loved the Word of God.

Memorize

The prophet Jeremiah memorized so much Scripture that he literally could not stop mentioning God or speaking in his name. How passionately do you want God's Word to burn within you? A good place to start might be to memorize the following:

> But if I say, "I will not mention him or speak any more in his name," his word is in my heart like a fire, a fire shut up in my bones. I am weary of holding it in; indeed, I cannot.
>
> Jeremiah 20:9

Pray for the same love for the Word as Jeremiah had.

Day four/synagogue: practicing faith in community

The Very Words of God

> They went to Capernaum, and when the Sabbath came, Jesus went into the synagogue and began to teach. The people were amazed at his teaching, because he taught them as one who had authority, not as the teachers of the law.
>
> Mark 1:21–22

Profile of the Synagogue

Originally, the synagogue was not a specific building but a place where God's people gathered in his presence around his living Word. It was sometimes called a place of prayer, because in the Jewish mind the verb translated *pray* means worship as well as prayer. Synagogue began before Solomon's temple was destroyed, but the practice became essential to the Jewish faith during the exile.

As exiled Jews returned to the land of Israel, they brought synagogue—the practice of coming together as a community to study and worship in God's presence—with them. By the first century in Israel, larger community buildings were built to serve as meeting places for synagogue. Soon the name *synagogue* was applied to the buildings where community study and worship of the Scriptures took place. So during Jesus' time, the synagogue was both a *place* and a *group* of people engaged in seeking God through the study of Scripture and prayer.

The synagogue in Chorazin

Synagogues played an important role in the lives of religious Jews who lived along the north and northwestern shores of the

Sea of Galilee. Although the Jews traveled to the temple in Jerusalem to worship three times a year, they worshiped regularly with family, friends, and neighbors in the local synagogue. The Torah scrolls were kept in the synagogue, so people went there to read and study the Scriptures and listen to the rabbis proclaim their interpretations of the text. Their children attended synagogue schools where they learned to read, write, and memorize the text. Thus the community worship, expressed in a handful of small synagogues in Galilee, contributed greatly to the disciples' preparation to follow Jesus, their Rabbi, and become like him in every way.

Bible Discovery

Discovering the Synagogue

The synagogue was central to the life of religious Jews in Galilee. It was where the faithful learned the Scriptures, how to interpret them, and how to obey God. So, how did Jesus and his disciples relate with the synagogue communities in Galilee? The Scriptures give us some surprising insights.

1. Matthew 4:23–25; 9:35; 12:9–13; 13:54–58; Mark 1:21–28; and Luke 4:14–30 are just a few of the passages that show Jesus participating in community worship in the synagogues of Galilee.

   a. When Jesus taught, how was his message received? What impact did his message have on the religious community? What do you think Jesus wanted to accomplish in the synagogues?

b. What else did Jesus do in the synagogues besides teach? What was his purpose in doing these things?

2. Who was Jairus, and what does his relationship with Jesus tell us about Jesus' relationship with the local synagogue? (See Luke 8:40–56.)

3. According to Acts 16:13–15; 17:1–4, what did Paul and Silas do on the Sabbath as they traveled through Macedonia? What do these (and many other passages) reveal about their involvement in the synagogue community? (Remember, a house of prayer is another way of saying synagogue.)

The Truth of the Matter

Christians today tend to think that the theology and teaching of the Pharisees was all wrong, but it was not. The Pharisees were faithful Jews who worked hard to obey God in all they did. That's why they had so many applications of Bible texts: they were trying to obey God! Jesus called some of the Pharisees hypocrites because they didn't practice their own teaching (and some of their own writings criticize this as well). Some other Pharisees were so set in their interpretations of the Scriptures that they refused to consider the interpretations of others—including the interpretations of Jesus. Despite their imperfections, the Pharisees made knowledge of the Scriptures and obedience to God top priorities in life.

Reflection

Although many Christians today think that Jesus called his disciples away from the Jewish faith and community, that is not the case. Jesus and his disciples continued to participate in community life, including synagogue worship, throughout his ministry. Even when his disciples went out into the world beyond Israel, they sought out and continued to be a part of the faith community of the synagogue. This is not to suggest that you must join a synagogue in order to follow Jesus, but active involvement in a faith community is necessary.

> How essential is your faith community in your walk with God? How does it help you focus on obeying God in all things at all times?

> Do you have a community of people with whom you share a mutual love for and delight in the Scriptures—people who encourage you to learn and study the Word of God? Remember, the reading of the Torah in the synagogue made the people dance with joy!

If a spiritual community is lacking in your life, ask God to lead you to such a community so that you can become more like Jesus.

Day Five/The Rabbi as Shepherd

The Very Words of God

I am the good shepherd; I know my sheep and my sheep know me—just as the Father knows me and I know the Father—and I lay down my life for the sheep.

John 10:14–15

Bible Discovery

Following the Good Shepherd

The image of the shepherd and his sheep is frequently used in Scripture as a metaphor for the relationship between God and his people. Not only that, God often chose shepherds to lead his people. Abram (Genesis 13:1–5), Moses (Exodus 3:1), and David (1 Samuel 17:14–15), for example, all were experienced shepherds. This image sent a powerful message to the people of Israel because even to this day a flock of sheep in Israel is dependent on the shepherd for survival. Israel is not a land of knee-high grass and abundant water. The shepherd must lead the sheep daily to graze on short tufts of grass on hillsides and to drink from widely scattered sources of water. Without the shepherd's leading, the flock would die.

The shepherd/sheep image describes the intimacy, dependence, obedience, and faithfulness that characterize the rabbi/disciple relationship as well. The rabbi walks ahead and leads his disciples by his voice. Just as sheep follow their shepherd without understanding why the shepherd leads where he leads, disciples follow the rabbi by faith, trusting him to lead them in the right way to the right place. Following the rabbi is just as much a matter of life and death for the disciple as it is for the sheep that follow the shepherd.

1. What do the following passages reveal about what a shepherd does for the sheep? What do these images say to a disciple who is following *the* Rabbi, the Good Shepherd? (See Psalm 78:52–55; Isaiah 40:10–11.)

2. Although the previous passages give us positive images of what the shepherd does for the flock, we can also learn much about the Good Shepherd by knowing how bad shepherds offend him. Ezekiel 34:1–16 paints this picture vividly. As you read this passage, ask yourself how much and in what ways the Good Shepherd loves his sheep. What difference would it make to a disciple (to you as a disciple) to be led by such a Rabbi?

3. In John 10:1–16, Jesus portrays himself as the Good Shepherd. What is he saying to his *talmidim* that will instruct and help them as they follow him and seek to be like him?

Did You Know?

In contrast to sheep who follow their shepherd, goats often wander on their own, away from the shepherd's chosen path, the "path of righteousness." Goats require extra attention from the shepherd because they think they know a better path.

In light of this, consider what Jesus taught in Matthew 25:31–46, particularly verses 32–34, 41: "He will separate the people one from another as a shepherd separates the sheep from the goats. He will put the sheep on his right and the goats on his left. Then the King will say to those on his right, 'Come, you who are blessed by my Father; take your inheritance, the kingdom prepared for you since the creation of the world.' ...

Then he will say to those on his left, 'Depart from me, you who are cursed, into the eternal fire.'" The key difference between the sheep and the goats is that the sheep obeyed the shepherd; they did what he would do. The goats, on the other hand, had no interest in what concerned the shepherd.

The sheep follow the shepherd's path, but the goats,
scattered across the hillside, choose their own way.

Reflection

Psalm 23:1–4 is a very familiar Scripture passage, but take a fresh look at it. Read it slowly and thoughtfully. Meditate on what it means in terms of Jesus being your Rabbi (Shepherd) and you being his disciple (sheep).

- As you live life, how carefully are you listening for the Good Shepherd's voice?
- How passionate is your desire to follow his every step, to be like him in every way?

- How much do you long to walk obediently in his paths of righteousness?
- How fully do you trust him to lead you when you do not know the way?
- Who will be with you when danger threatens?

If the Good Shepherd is your Rabbi, what qualities do you need to cultivate in your life to be a true disciple? When he says, "Come," will you follow?

Memorize

I am the good shepherd; I know my sheep and my sheep know me—just as the Father knows me and I know the Father—and I lay down my life for the sheep.

John 10:14–15

Session 2

when the rabbi says "go"

In the previous session, we learned some of what it meant to be a rabbi, an honored teacher whose life revolved around following God, knowing the Holy Scriptures, and making disciples. In this session, we will focus more attention on the disciples—the motivation, commitment, and training of the young men who devoted themselves to walking in the footsteps of the rabbi so that they might learn to follow God. We will discover some of the lessons Jesus taught them on the ancient paths he once walked. And we will stand with him and hear his final command to his disciples, "Go, and make disciples ... teaching them to obey ...."

For a moment, reflect back to when Jesus walked along the shore of the Sea of Galilee and said to some fishermen, "Come, follow me," and they left everything to do so. Now fast-forward to a sunny, spring day on a rocky, uninhabited hillside above the small Galilean villages of Capernaum and Gennesareth and below the village of Chorazin. Beautiful red flowers sway in the breeze. Waves on the Sea of Galilee sparkle in the distance. Jesus, the beloved and now resurrected Rabbi, stands with his eleven disciples.

They disciples had walked about 110 miles from Jerusalem to this place where Jesus had told them to go. Jesus met them there, in Galilee, where for a few years they had shared so much together. When he spoke, his challenge stirred their hearts as it continues to stir our hearts today: "All authority in heaven and on earth has been given to me. Therefore go and make disciples of all nations, baptizing them in the name of the Father and of the Son and of the Holy Spirit, and teaching them to obey everything I have commanded you. And surely I am with you always, to the very end of the age" (Matthew 28:18–20). Jesus made their mission clear: "Go ... make disciples of all nations ... baptizing ... teaching them to obey everything." Then he ascended to heaven.

In these two commissions, Jesus called each of his own to a life of discipleship. "Come," he invites. "Go," he commands. And his disciples did both.

The disciples were ready to fulfill their mission. Jesus the Messiah, who is much more than an ordinary rabbi, had prepared them well. They had learned to obey everything their Rabbi taught and literally followed him everywhere he went. Although their progress was slow and imperfect, they had learned to follow Jesus' walk—his obedience to God's commands. They had learned to walk as he walked and to teach as he taught. And they had learned how to make other disciples who would do the same.

Discipleship is essential to the message of Jesus. Being a disciple and making disciples is at the heart of the movement Jesus came to create. Let's explore some ways by which Jesus prepared his disciples, primarily in the small province of Galilee, to take the message of the kingdom of heaven to a very different and challenging pagan world.

opening Thoughts (4 minutes)

The Very Words of God

Then Jesus came to them and said, "All authority in heaven and on earth has been given to me. Therefore go and make disciples of all nations, baptizing them in the name of the Father and of the Son and of the Holy Spirit, and teaching them to obey everything I have commanded you. And surely I am with you always, to the very end of the age."

Matthew 28:18–20

Think About It

What kind of person do you think would be a good disciple? What personal qualities, knowledge, and experience make a good disciple?

DVD Notes (21 minutes)

Herod's temple to Caesar

Jesus teaches a lesson for the future

Going across to Bethsaida

What was Peter thinking?

Chorazin vs. Beth Shean (Scythopolis)

DVD Highlights (4 minutes)

1. How did Jesus use the question regarding paying tribute to Caesar to address the claim of deity made by the Roman emperor, Tiberius? What impact do you think that teaching had on Jesus' disciples?

2. From the short clips you've seen about Jesus' life, teaching, and interaction with religious leaders, what specific things do you think his disciples—his *talmidim*—learned that helped prepare them for their future ministry?

3. What did Jesus' ordinary disciples have to believe about God, his Word, and their calling as disciples in order to even think about making disciples in a city like Beth Shean (Scythopolis)?

Did You Know?

God began preparing Jesus' disciples for their future ministry at an early age! Jewish boys and girls in Galilee began *Beth Sefer*, the equivalent of elementary education, at age four or five. A Torah teacher (teacher of the law) taught them to read and memorize the Torah. At about age thirteen, the very best male students advanced to *Beth Midrash*, while the majority of boys ended their formal schooling and began working in the family trade. By this age, girls had completed their formal schooling and remained at home.

Although some Jews of the day appeared to disrespect the Galileans, be careful not to underestimate how well educated they were. The Jews in Galilee generally had access to the Scriptures only in their local synagogue, so they memorized Scripture throughout their lifetimes because they were determined to know and live by the Word of God and to pass on their faith to their children. They were intensely spiritual people, and even those who did not advance to further study and interpretation of the Torah and the Prophets already had memorized far more Scripture than most Christians know today.

small Group Bible Discovery and Discussion (18 minutes)

Jesus Chooses His Disciples

In the culture of Jesus' day, a young man who had been an outstanding *Beth Midrash* student and had the desire to be a *talmid* would ask to follow a rabbi and study with him. The rabbi would get to know the potential *talmid*, test him, and evaluate him based on his knowledge, commitment, character, and other desirable qualities. Then the rabbi would accept or reject him as his *talmid*.

In contrast to this tradition, Jesus personally chose each of his disciples. The Gospels record *no* example of Jesus accepting anyone who came to him and requested to be his disciple, although several asked about following him. In fact, before he called his disciples Jesus had been teaching and building a reputation in the communities of Galilee and beyond. People had been seeking him out and following him, but not as *talmidim*. So when Jesus actually chose his *talmidim*, at least several of them may have spent considerable time with him prior to his call.

1. The following passages show us how Jesus called several of his disciples. Read these passages together and discuss the insights you gain into what it means to be a disciple of Jesus.

    a. Matthew 4:18–22

        What were Peter, Andrew, James, and John doing when Jesus called them to be his disciples?

        In light of how first-century synagogue schools operated, what can we conclude from the fact that these four young men were working rather than studying in *Beth Midrash*?

        What would have been their religious standing in the community? How do you think they must have felt when Jesus invited them to be his *talmidim*?

    b. Matthew 9:9

        How unusual would it have been for a rabbi to call a tax collector to be his disciple?

        What would have been Matthew's status in the religious community? How do you think he must have felt when Jesus invited him to be his *talmid*?

c. John 1:35 – 51

Who did some of the young men who later became Jesus'
disciples follow before Jesus called them to follow him? What
does this reveal about their faith?

What did these young men believe was true about Jesus?
Why? What was their immediate response to what they
believed?

Did You Know?

Generations before Jesus chose his disciples, the prophet
Jeremiah had predicted that God would use fishermen to call his
people back to him! The text (Jeremiah 16:16) reads, "'But now I
will send for many fishermen,' declares the LORD, 'and they will
catch them.'" What do you think the Galileans, including the
disciples, must have thought when Jesus called several fishermen to be his disciples?

---

2. Read Luke 5:1 – 11.

a. What was the lifestyle of Galilean fishermen? Which personal qualities and strengths refined by the work of fishing would equip them well for the future work Jesus had in
mind for them? How might their understanding of fishing
make them better disciples?

b. How did Peter respond when Jesus told them to throw out
    their nets one more time? Why do you think he agreed to do
    something that by all reason and experience seemed futile?
    What was he beginning to realize about Jesus, about him-
    self, and how did that realization affect him?

c. What new goal in life did Jesus give to Peter and his
    companions?

Data File

From Where Did Jesus Call His Disciples?

Matthew—Most likely from the vicinity of Capernaum (Matthew 4:13; 9:1, 9–13).

Simon the Zealot—Possibly from Gamla, the center of the
Zealot movement, northeast of the Sea of Galilee (Luke 6:15).

Peter and Andrew—The fishing village of Bethsaida (Matthew
4:18–20; John 1:44).

James and John—Fishing partners with Peter and Andrew, most
likely from Bethsaida (Matthew 4:18–22; Luke 5:1–10).

Philip—Bethsaida (John 1:43–44; 12:21).

Nathanael (also called Bartholomew)—From Cana, northeast
of Nazareth (John 1:43–51; 21:2).

Judas Iscariot—Apparently the only non-Galilean disciple.
(*Iscariot* is Aramaic, meaning "man from Kerioth." Kerioth was a village in Judea near Hebron known for its Zealot
sympathies.)

Thomas, **Thaddeus** (also called Judas, son of James), **James** son
of Alphaeus—Uncertain; believed to be from Galilee.

3. Why do you think Jesus' eleven disciples could go out and change the world, yet nearly one billion believers today seem to be so ineffective? What gave the disciples the confidence, motivation, and passion to be like Jesus and make a difference in their world?

Think About It

You can say, "I *will not be* a disciple of Jesus." But Jesus believes in you and your potential to be his disciple. That is why he chose you (John 15:16)! Therefore, it is not true that you *cannot be* his disciple.

Ray Vander Laan

4. What are some of the things we believe about Jesus, ourselves, and our faith that hinder us from being true disciples?

What do we need to change in order to be the *talmidim* Jesus has called everyone who follows him to be?

> ### Worth Observing ...
> #### *The Journey of Discipleship*
>
> 1. Jesus the Rabbi called his disciples (Matthew 4:19).
> 2. They decided to follow him (Matthew 4:20).
> 3. Disciples lived with Jesus and learned from him (Mark 3:14; Matthew 5:1–2).
> 4. Slowly the disciples became more like Jesus (Luke 9:1–6; 10:1–7).
> 5. Disciples sometimes failed (Luke 22:54–57).
> 6. When they failed, Jesus forgave them (John 21:15–17).
> 7. Jesus called them again to follow him (John 21:19).

ꜰɑɪᴛʜ ʟᴇssᴏɴ (7 minutes)

God Uses All Kinds of Faithful People

Jesus chose ordinary Galileans, trained them to be his disciples, and sent them out to do his ministry. This may seem like a strange choice to us, but Scripture records many other times when God chose seemingly weak, less educated, or otherwise unworthy people to fulfill his purposes. Review the following examples, and read more about the person if you are unfamiliar with his/her story.

"Unworthy" person	The work God used him/her to accomplish
Sarah—a barren woman	Becomes Isaac's mother, continues the line into which the Messiah would be born (Genesis 18, 21)
Joseph—a slave	Saves God's people from famine (Genesis 37–48)
Moses—a wanted criminal with a speech impediment	Leads God's people out of Egypt (Exodus 2–13)

Rahab—a prostitute	Saves God's people, and because of her obedience and faith is included in Jesus' family line (Joshua 2, 6; Matthew 1)
Ruth of Moab—a pagan who was forbidden to be with God's people	Preserves the family line into which David and Jesus would be born (Deuteronomy 23:3; Ruth; Matthew 1)
Gideon—a fearful farmer	Leads God's people to victory over the Midianites (Judges 6–7)
David—the youngest son	Preserves God's people by defeating Goliath and the Philistines; archetypal king of God's people; forerunner of the Messiah (1 Samuel 16–17; Matthew 1)
Mary—an unmarried virgin from a tiny village	Chosen to be Jesus' mother by the miracle of God (Luke 2; Matthew 1)

1. Think about why these people would have been considered unworthy to do God's bidding, then take note of the character and qualities they demonstrated as they obeyed God's call.

2. Read 1 Corinthians 1:26–31 and consider the effects of God's choice of "foolish" and "weak" things.

   a. Why does God choose unlikely people, and why is it difficult to believe that God can do great things through them?

b. How do God's values, as reflected in this passage, influence how you perceive your worth in God's eyes and your ability to be the disciple he has called you to be? What adjustments might you need to make in how you view yourself and how you follow him?

3. Jesus chose the unlikely, but they were *talmidim*—living and learning with him twenty-four hours a day, seven days a week. What kind of discipleship is based primarily on an hour or two of teaching a week?

4. If you do not think you are smart enough or good enough to be a disciple of Jesus, why is it important to remember who Jesus called to follow him, how he called them, what he believed about them, and what they accomplished? In what ways does his example feed your passion, faith, desire, and confidence to follow God at all costs?

closing (1 minute)

Read the following verse aloud. Then pray, asking God to use this session and the coming ones to give you a greater passion to become a true disciple of Jesus.

Memorize

This is what the LORD says: "Let not the wise man boast of his wisdom or the strong man boast of his strength or the rich man boast of his riches, but let him who boasts boast about this: that he understands and knows me, that I am the LORD, who exercises kindness, justice and righteousness on earth, for in these I delight" declares the LORD.

Jeremiah 9:23–24

walking with the rabbi day by day
In-Depth Personal Study Sessions

day one/how do you follow god?

The Very Words of God

Our Father in heaven, hallowed be your name, your kingdom come, your will be done on earth as it is in heaven. Give us today our daily bread. Forgive us our debts, as we also have forgiven our debtors. And lead us not into temptation, but deliver us from the evil one.

                                                          Matthew 6:9–13

Data File
What Did It Mean to Follow God?

The opening scene of the DVD segment at Omrit, the temple Herod built in honor of the Roman emperor, goes to the heart of what it means to be a disciple of Jesus—how do you follow God? We know that Jesus spent years teaching and showing his disciples how to follow God, but we may not realize how crucial a question this was for Jews at the time. How to follow God was a highly debated topic. Consider just a few of the varied ways that Jews followed God during the time of Jesus and his disciples:

Paul Followed God

Saul (later renamed Paul) was an exceptional student of the Scriptures. He was a highly qualified *talmid* who had studied under Gamaliel, one of the greatest ancient sages and leader of the Hillel school. So Paul knew Scripture, was trained in the rabbinic system, and was absolutely convinced that the way to follow God was to persecute the early Christians. It took a divine encounter with Jesus (which must have happened just down the road from the temple at Omrit) for Paul to recognize his blindness and open his eyes to how God was fulfilling the very Scriptures he knew so well. (See Galatians 1:11–17; Acts 22:3–16.)

The Zealots Followed God

The Zealot movement was founded in Gamla, a town on a mountaintop above the northeastern corner of the Sea of Galilee. For nearly a hundred years, the Zealots fought against the emperors' authority and longed for a messiah who would raise up a great army and destroy the Roman overlords. Their violence against the Romans was motivated by far more than a desire to be free from oppression, however. They were totally devoted to serving God and believed it was impossible to serve the Romans and be faithful to God too. So their resistance to Rome was rooted in how they believed they must follow God. Notice the top priorities of their creed: (1) God alone was to be served; (2) neither Rome nor Herod was a legitimate authority; (3) taxes were to be paid only to God; and (4) serving Rome, whether by choice or as a slave, violated God's supreme authority!

The Pharisees and Rabbis Followed God

Contrary to the understanding of many Christians today, the Pharisees sought to follow God in all of life. That's why they sought to apply Scripture to every detail of life. They didn't want to get any of it wrong! Each rabbi taught his disciples how Torah should be obeyed, meaning they taught how to follow God according to their best interpretation of the Scriptures. For a disciple to obey his rabbi's teaching on how to follow God was to take on "the yoke of Torah" (see Matthew 11:28–30).

So the Pharisees had multiple purposes in mind when they asked Jesus about whether or not to give tribute to Caesar (Matthew 22:15–22). They were hoping he would say something they could use against him before the Roman or temple authorities. But part of what they were asking was where Jesus landed on the "How do you follow God?" question. They wanted to know whose side he was on. Jesus, who knew the hearts of his questioners and the heart of his message, gave an amazing response that silenced his critics and taught his disciples a fundamental truth.

**Denarius of Tiberius with the inscription,
"The worshiped son of a worshiped God."**

Bible Discovery

Follow God and God Alone

Jesus' response to the question of whether or not one should pay tribute to Caesar, which meant to acknowledge the emperor's divine superiority, communicated a powerful message to Jesus' disciples as well as to his critics. (See Matthew 22:18–21.) Without exactly saying so, Jesus clearly communicated that Caesar was not God! Why was this important? The sovereign lordship of God as eternal king was the fundamental premise of everything that Jesus taught! God's exclusive authority has always been the reason for following him and obeying him in everything.

When Jesus taught, he often used the phrase "the kingdom of heaven." In Scripture, this phrase can refer to paradise or the life to come, but it also had a special meaning for the Jews in Jesus' day that related to following God. You will better understand how to follow God if you understand how Jesus used this phrase to communicate to his audience.

1. The kingdom of heaven concept originated when God delivered the Israelites from the Egyptians. Even the Egyptians recognized God's power at work in the plagues upon Egypt (Exodus 8:19). In Exodus 19:3–8, God reminded the people of how he had acted in power to deliver them from Egypt and clearly stated what he expected of them.

   What kind of kingdom did God say they would be if they obeyed him? What did the people agree to do? What were they accepting and affirming by agreeing to obey?

2. What did the Israelites do after they crossed the Red Sea and saw the Egyptian army swept away? What conclusion had they reached about God's power? How did they acclaim his rule? (See Exodus 14:29–15:18.)

3. It is one thing to see God's power and acclaim his rule, but it is another to accept his rule in one's own life. The Jews who remembered the exodus would take on obedience to the kingdom of heaven by seeking to obey God in all things so that his reign would become a reality in their lives. Moses first expressed this allegiance in Deuteronomy 6:4–12.

    In what ways were the Israelites to obey God and thereby make God's kingdom a reality on earth?

4. How do we know that allegiance to the kingdom of heaven as expressed in the *Shema* (Deuteronomy 6:4–5) was very much on the minds of religious Jews in Jesus' day? (See Mark 12:28–34.)

    How was God's great power revealed in Jesus' ministry? (See Luke 11:20.)

    How did the people acclaim Jesus? Is acclamation enough? (See Matthew 7:21–23.)

    What else is required to show allegiance to the kingdom of heaven? (See Matthew 7:21.)

5. How essential do you think Jesus considers obedience to be in the kingdom of heaven? (See Matthew 21:28–32.) What does this understanding of the kingdom of heaven require of you?

For Greater Understanding ...
The Kingdom of Heaven or the Kingdom of God?

Jesus often taught about the "kingdom of heaven" or the "kingdom of God." Matthew alone records thirty-one times when Jesus spoke of the kingdom of heaven (*Malchut Shemayim*, Hebrew). And he referred to the kingdom of God four times in Matthew, fourteen times in Mark, thirty-one times in Luke, and two times in John.

But why does Scripture record "kingdom of heaven" in some cases and "kingdom of God" in others? Do they refer to the same thing?

Jewish people had fear and awe for the name of God, so they rarely said his name aloud (Exodus 20:7; Daniel 4:25). Even Jesus used titles such as *Father, God,* or *Mighty One* rather than saying the name of God. Jewish people often used the word *heaven* to refer to God (Mark 11:30; Luke 15:18). Therefore, "kingdom of heaven" doesn't simply refer to the life to come but can also refer to the "kingdom of God," meaning the kingdom over which God rules.

Reflection

Most likely you are familiar with the Lord's Prayer found in Matthew 6:9 – 13 (also Luke 11:2 – 4). Possibly you have even memorized it. Read this prayer again (preferably aloud), and focus on the meaning of its individual phrases in light of what the disciples would have understood about the kingdom of heaven:

Our Father in heaven,
hallowed be your name,
your kingdom come,
your will be done on earth as it is in heaven.
Give us today our daily bread.
Forgive us our debts, as we also have forgiven our debtors.
And lead us not into temptation, but deliver us from the evil one.

Remember, there is a connection between doing God's will and the coming of his kingdom: God's kingdom comes as his will is done. What is our part in this process? What must you do in your life in order for God's kingdom to come?

Now read the prayer again and focus on the meaning of its individual phrases in your life and your walk with God. What are you affirming as you read? To what are you making a commitment? What do you desire to see happen as you pray this prayer?

In what ways is this prayer a model for following God in your daily life?

Did You Know?

How to Experience the Kingdom of Heaven

- Recognize God and God alone as sovereign Lord.
- Accept his reign by obeying him in all things.
- Establish the kingdom of heaven by doing his will.

Day Two/Follow the Rabbi to Become Like the Rabbi

The Very Words of God

A student is not above his teacher, but everyone who is fully trained will be like his teacher.

Luke 6:40

Bible Discovery

Follow to Become: The Core of Discipleship Training

The relationship between a first-century rabbi and his disciples was unique. It was very intense and personal—like a dynamic father/son relationship. As a disciple followed his rabbi, he would get to know him as well or better than his own family. In time, the walk of the disciple would become like the walk of his rabbi.

1. Each of the following passages describes some aspect of what it meant to follow Jesus. Read each one and carefully note what Jesus expected his "disciples-in-training" to do and be.

   a. Mark 3:13–19

   b. Mark 8:34–35

   c. Matthew 19:21–30

Fact File
What Jesus Meant When He Said, "Follow Me!"

The Greek word *akolouthein* (based on the Hebrew to "walk after"), which appears more than eighty-five times in the New Testament, captures the command a rabbi would give to a potential disciple. It was an invitation to join him wherever he went and especially to do whatever he did. As the disciples followed Jesus, they walked hundreds of miles and faced danger, difficulty, and opposition. Often they did not know where they were going, how long it would take, how difficult it would be, or whether they could do it. Through everything, they needed to learn to trust their rabbi with their lives without being able to evaluate their capability to do what he asked. They needed to believe that he knew where he was leading, had a purpose in doing so, and would never lead them into a situation that they, by God's grace, could not handle.

2. People responded to Jesus in different ways, and many were unwilling to follow him. Read Luke 9:57–62 and note the kinds of obstacles that prevented some people from following Jesus. In what way do these obstacles still trip up potential disciples?

3. The point of following Jesus, as expressed in 1 John 2:3–6, is to obey and learn to walk as Jesus walked—to become like him. So part of the disciples' training included going out to preach the kingdom of God just as Jesus had done. Jesus sent out the twelve as well as a larger group of seventy-two followers. Read about their experiences in Luke 9:1–6; 10:1–9, 17–20.

a. What happened to Jesus' followers after they went out to do what he had prepared and trained them to do? In what ways were they becoming like Jesus?

b. How did Jesus respond to their faithfulness and success? How might Jesus respond whenever a disciple follows, obeys, and becomes more like him?

4. Despite their human failings, Jesus' disciples eventually became very much like their Rabbi. They walked as he walked, and when they were fully trained, they became like him. Read Acts 4:5 – 13; 5:12 – 16 and list the ways the disciples had become like their Rabbi.

Walking with Jesus Today

For a disciple in Jesus' day, there was no shortcut to becoming like the rabbi in his walk with God. The rabbi expected a disciple to be with him all the time. Although Jesus is not with us in the flesh as he was with the twelve disciples, his expectation for us to follow him, walk with him, and become like him has not changed. Consider some of the ways in which we can spend time walking with Jesus our Rabbi so that we can become like him. The following ideas will help you get started:

- Spend time with his body, the community of faith.
- Keep the images of how Jesus walked fresh in your mind by reading the Gospels regularly—perhaps once a month for the rest of your life.
- Read the entire Bible every three years—or more frequently. (The Bible is the Word of God that points to and leads from the Messiah, so it's also part of becoming like Jesus.)
- Memorize as much Scripture as you can. You might start by memorizing one of the Gospels.

Reflection

What must be an absolute priority in a disciple's life if he or she is to obey Jesus' command to "follow me?" Are you willing to accept his call, without knowing what such obedience will entail? Why or why not?

Have you ever followed anyone with total trust? If so, what was it like? What challenges do you face in seeking to trust and follow Jesus completely?

If you were to use the amount of time you spend in the Word of God as the measure of your commitment to being a disciple, how committed are you to following Jesus and becoming like him?

In what ways might you expect to change—in your heart, in your life, in your relationships with others—if you were to make becoming like Jesus your top priority? How would your life be different if you were to become more like Jesus?

Profile of a People Who Were Determined to Follow God

Jesus grew up and spent his ministry among the most religious Jews in the world. Galileans were known for their great reverence for Scripture and their passionate desire to be faithful to it in every aspect of daily life. The people of Galilee knew Scripture by memory, debated its application with enthusiasm, loved God with all their heart, soul, and strength (Deuteronomy 6:5), and trained their children to do the same. Their great desire to follow God translated into vibrant religious communities whose synagogues echoed with debates and discussions about keeping the Torah. As a result, Galilee produced more famous rabbis than any other region in the world.

Jesus fit into this culture perfectly. God had prepared an environment where Jesus would find disciples and followers who understood and would join his new movement. Galilee provided exactly the context Jesus needed in which to present his message of the kingdom of heaven. The spiritual culture of Galilee also helps us understand the great faith and courage of Jesus' disciples, who took Jesus' message to the world. Their courage, methods, and complete devotion to God and his Word were born and cultivated in the Galilean communities in which they grew up.

Day Three/walk in obedience

The Very Words of God

If you love me, you will obey what I command.... If anyone loves me, he will obey my teaching. My Father will love him, and we will come to him and make our home with him.

John 14:15, 23

Bible Discovery

Is Obedience Absolutely Necessary?

God gives us salvation by grace alone; no amount of obedience can ever earn it for us. But that doesn't mean obedience is not necessary for those who love God and call themselves his disciples. The following study of Scripture will help those who want to walk with Jesus put obedience in its rightful perspective.

Think About It

A walk (lifestyle) without God is a tragedy.

Ray Vander Laan

---

1. You're already familiar with it, but take one more look at 1 John 2:3–6. Do you see any way that obedience and walking as Jesus walked can be thought of as optional for a disciple of Jesus? What is the identifying mark of a person who truly follows Jesus?

2. Jesus not only taught obedience to God, he also lived it. Read John 8:28–31 and note what Jesus said regarding his own obedience in action and in words.

a. What did Jesus do and say, and what was the result in his relationship with God?

b. What did Jesus teach those who believed in him about obedience to his teachings? What do you think we can expect when we obey his teachings and please the Father in all things?

3. We tend to underestimate the importance of obedience in the life of a follower of Jesus. In what ways do the following passages contradict that assumption?

a. Read Luke 6:46–49. What question does Jesus ask, and in what tone do you think he asked it? What did he say obedience is like, and what does it accomplish? What are the results when obedience is lacking?

b. Read John 14:19–24. Who does Jesus say loves him? In this passage, Jesus explains much about obedience, relationships, and the results. What relationships exist among Jesus, the Father, obedience, and love? (These relationships are so interrelated it might be helpful to diagram them so you clearly see the picture Jesus presented.)

c. Read John 15:9–11. What are the results of obedience?
    Describe in terms of the world you live in how different life
    would be if you walked in obedience—or did not.

Did You Know?

During biblical times, people often walked long distances.

- Abraham and his family walked to the Promised Land.
- The people of Israel walked out of Egypt to Sinai, walked
  for forty years in the wilderness, and eventually walked
  to the Promised Land.
- The people of Israel walked to captivity in Babylon and
  seventy years later walked back.
- In Jesus' time, religious Jews who lived in Galilee walked
  more than 110 miles one way to Jerusalem for worship
  three times a year (Deuteronomy 16:16). Many did this
  joyfully year after year because of their devotion to God
  (Luke 2:42).
- Jesus walked throughout Galilee and beyond, and Paul
  must have been one of the greatest walkers ever (more
  than ten thousand miles during his mission tours
  alone).

No wonder the Bible has more than three hundred references
to walking! Walking was such an important part of life that the
practice of expressing truth concretely, in story or word picture,
led to images of walking becoming a significant metaphor for a
person's life or lifestyle. Thus in biblical terminology, the way
you live is your "walk." The passage through time is your walk
on the path. Life is a journey—a walk with or without God.

So when Jesus called his disciples to walk after him, he meant it both literally and figuratively. "Walk after [follow] me and learn to walk as I walk," he said, in effect, "then make disciples, calling them to follow [walk after] you as you follow me."

Reflection

Think about your understanding of obedience in the Christian life. To what extent is obedience emphasized in the Christian community in which you are involved? What is it you have been taught to obey and why? In what way might your understanding of what obedience is, its importance, and what it requires differ from what you have just explored in the Scriptures?

What happens when a person's faith practice is based solely on *knowing* the right things instead of also *doing* the right things on the right path?

James 2:14–26 can be a confusing passage for Christians today. How does understanding the context of discipleship as Jesus taught it help clarify the meaning of this passage for you?

How serious is your personal commitment to "walk as Jesus walked"? In what specific ways does your walk need to follow his more closely? What are you looking forward to as you take those steps?

Memorize

> *If you love me, you will obey what I command.... If anyone loves me, he will obey my teaching. My Father will love him, and we will come to him and make our home with him.*
>
> John 14:15, 23

Day Four/What Was Peter Thinking?

The Very Words of God

> *"Lord, if it's you," Peter replied, "tell me to come to you on the water."*
>
> *"Come," he said.*
>
> *Then Peter got down out of the boat, walked on the water and came toward Jesus.*
>
> Matthew 14:28–29

Bible Discovery

Pushing the Limits of Devotion

You don't have to know much about the disciples to know the story of Peter's nighttime walk with Jesus on the Sea of Galilee. Chances are you've heard a variety of explanations as to what happened that night and the lessons learned. But let's look at this story again through the eyes of a *talmid* who is completely devoted to becoming like his Rabbi and has a consuming passion to follow him wherever he goes.

1. Read Mark 6:45–50 and John 6:18–19. This event happened immediately after Jesus fed the five thousand. Scriptural details and historical tradition indicate that the disciples probably started their boat ride west of Bethsaida in the general vicinity of Capernaum.

   a. What do you imagine the mood of the disciples was as they started out toward Bethsaida? What might they have talked about? What might they have been thinking about Jesus and why he was not with them? In what ways do you think their frame of mind might have changed during the night?

b. What is the only recorded activity that Jesus did without his disciples [hint: it's described here], and what does this reveal about the Rabbi's commitment to his *talmidim* and the need for time alone with God?

c. For how long did the disciples row before Jesus went out to them? (NOTE: the "fourth watch" is between 3 and 6 a.m.) What had Jesus been doing as the disciples struggled on the sea?

d. How did the disciples react when they first saw Jesus? How might their location (on the abyss) as well as their difficulties during the storm have intensified their response? If you had been in the boat, what would you have been thinking about following the Rabbi at that moment?

2. Read Matthew 14:26–33. Keep in mind that the disciples were probably not at their best when Jesus showed up. Within a few hours they had seen Jesus perform an amazing miracle, spent hours rowing in heavy seas, faced grave danger in the storm, and thought they had seen a ghost. So we can assume that they were physically, mentally, and emotionally exhausted.

a. How much do you think Peter thought about what he was going to do before he did it? What does this tell you about what was most important to him?

b. What do you think motivated Peter to take the action he did? What in the text indicates that this was his motivation? How badly did he want to be like Jesus?

c. If you had talked to Peter earlier in the day, do you think he would have said that he could walk on water? What, then, enabled him to do it?

d. What do you think caused Peter to doubt? In what did he lose confidence?

e. After things calmed down, how did Jesus' *talmidim* respond? How do you think this event affected their walk with God?

Data File
Fishing on the Sea of Galilee

This freshwater lake in northeastern Israel is nearly thirteen miles long, more than seven miles wide, and up to four hundred feet deep. It is fed by the Jordan River and runoff from winter snow, and even today remains a key source of fresh water for Israel. The water's surface is seven hundred feet below sea level, but most of the lake is surrounded by steep hills. On the east side (today's Golan Heights), the hills rise up to fifteen hundred feet above sea level. When weather conditions are right, this topography can create sudden, severe storms on the Sea of Galilee.

These storms only added to the reputation of the Sea of Galilee during New Testament times as being a place of evil and chaos. Traditionally, the Jews have feared the sea as a symbol of the abyss, the place where evil spirits live. So, although fish were plentiful, fishing was not a major industry at that time. This cultural background helps us better understand the disciples' reaction when Jesus stilled the storm (Matthew 14:22–32; Mark 4:35–41). It may also explain why even today this lake remains free of piers, condominiums, and resorts that are typically found around beautiful lakes in other parts of the world.

**The Sea of Galilee and the Golan Heights (the Decapolis in Jesus' day)
as seen from the hills above Capernaum**

Fishermen on the Sea of Galilee today still catch the same kinds of fish and use the same types of nets and small boats that the disciples would have used. A first-century boat recently discovered in the mud of the Sea of Galilee is twenty-six feet long and seven and a half feet wide, and would have had a small sail and oars. The sides of these small boats are low to make it easier for fishermen to cast their nets over the edge and pull them back in. Waves do not have to be high to threaten a boat's occupants.

A replica of a first-century fishing boat

Reflection

Scripture reveals that the disciples rowed quite a distance in the storm—at least three miles (John 6:19; Mark 6:48). Why do you think Jesus allowed them to struggle so long and hard?

Have you ever been "rowing against the wind" in your attempt to follow Jesus? What did you think Jesus was doing while you struggled? How does this event in the lives of Jesus' disciples change your perception of what might be happening when you face difficulties?

What do you think all twelve *talmidim* learned that night about the effort and commitment required to be like their Rabbi? How badly did they want to be like Jesus after that night?

In which area(s) do you fear that you are unable to follow your Rabbi? Does that stop you from trying? Why or why not? What do you believe Jesus is willing to do if you take that risky step? Will you take it? Will you get out of the boat?

Day five/Make Talmidim

The Very Words of God

"All authority in heaven and on earth has been given to me. Therefore go and make disciples of all nations, baptizing them in the name of the Father and of the Son and of the Holy Spirit, and teaching them to obey everything I have commanded you. And surely I am with you always, to the very end of the age."

Matthew 28:18–20

Bible Discovery

Jesus Prepared Talmidim to Make Talmidim

The disciples were in Jerusalem when Jesus was crucified and rose from the dead, but before Jesus ascended into heaven he had them walk back to Galilee. There, on the same hills above the Sea of Galilee where he had taught them how to *be* disciples, Jesus commissioned them to *make* disciples. Then, he had them walk back to Jerusalem to await the coming of the Holy Spirit at Pentecost. So even during these last preparatory events, the disciples were still walking in obedience to their Rabbi. Once their preparation was complete, they would walk even farther!

Israel of Jesus' time

1. Read Matthew 28:16–20.

   a. As Jesus commissioned his disciples to make disciples, what impact do you think the setting in Galilee had on them? What do you think they remembered of their training experiences in the area? How might that setting have encouraged them in their future ministry?

   b. Where did Jesus tell his *talmidim* to go? How much traveling had the disciples done up to that time? What do you think they thought when Jesus told them where to make disciples?

   c. What four things did Jesus command the disciples to *do*?

   d. What is significant, in light of the Rabbi/*talmidim* relationship, about Jesus' final words: that he would always be with them?

What Do You Think?

Why did Jesus command his disciples to, "Go and make *disciples*?" He could have told them to make converts or church members, to do evangelism, or the like. Is there a difference between a Christian and a disciple of Jesus?

Does it seem to you that many Christians today have forgotten the *discipleship* part of Jesus' commission? What has happened to our desire:

- To follow Jesus the Rabbi and passionately seek to become like him?
- To immerse ourselves in Scripture?
- To seek the fire of the Spirit?
- To teach and live as if the kingdom of heaven is near?

By failing to be *talmidim*, how much of the thrill of being part of God's great work are we missing?

2. Although he was not one of the disciples who walked with Jesus through the hills and villages of Galilee, Paul was certainly a *talmid*. He had two rabbis—the great Gamaliel and the greatest of all, Jesus. Read 1 Corinthians 4:16–17; 11:1–2; Philippians 3:17–20; and 1 Thessalonians 1:4–7 and notice how Paul taught those who followed him. What did he say over and over again? Why did he ask believers to do this?

To help establish in your mind the biblical model for making disciples, list all of the ways in which Paul imitated his Rabbi as he poured his life into making disciples.

Worth Observing ...
Making Disciples the First-Century Way

Jesus' disciples went out and made disciples just as Jesus had taught them. The scriptural record of their work helps us see the practical side of the process. Note what each of these passages reveals about the process of making disciples:

- Acts 6:1–7—Fulfilling the ministry of the Word of God by making disciples was a top priority.
- Acts 14:21–28—They not only continued teaching, they strengthened and encouraged disciples to remain true to the faith.
- Acts 19:8–10—They taught boldly and faithfully, in this case, teaching daily for two years!
- Acts 21:15–16—They cared for and supported one another.

Reflection

Jesus' disciples had to choose to follow him and learn the path of discipleship *before* they could go out and make disciples. It is no different for those who would be Jesus' disciples today. We can *make* disciples only when we *are* disciples. Are you willing to be a disciple of Jesus?

In light of how Jesus prepared his disciples for ministry, what is God doing in your life to prepare you to make disciples? How closely are you walking in his steps? Is your preparation sufficient that you should be making disciples? Why or why not?

Think about what it would look like to be a *talmid* of Jesus in your world. What does becoming a disciple involve?

How must your life change if you truly dedicate yourself to being like Jesus the Rabbi?

What is required for you to make disciples who will become like Jesus as they imitate you?

How committed are you to going into your world and making disciples? Why?

The Wisdom of the Rabbis

Do not live without a rabbi or die without a disciple.

Memorize

Follow my example, as I follow the example of Christ. I praise you for remembering me in everything and for holding to the teachings, just as I passed them on to you.

1 Corinthians 11:1–2

Session 3

The presence of God: A counter-cultural community

Jesus' disciples understood that the goal of those who followed Jesus was not simply to "seek converts" but to make disciples. They knew how to make disciples from among the Jews in Galilee who knew all about God and Scripture and were already deeply committed to obeying God. Making disciples there meant showing that Jesus was the next great step in God's redeeming work. It meant helping people understand how to live according to Jesus' interpretation of Scripture and his teachings. But after Jesus' ascension, his disciples faced new and compelling challenges.

What would happen when the way Jesus modeled disciple-making ran head-on into the Hellenistic view of the world outside of Galilee, the world into which Jesus sent his disciples? How would they make disciples among people in Asia Minor who knew little about the Jewish God? Among people who already worshiped an array of gods and seemed quite happy? Among people who had virtually no sense of sin or need for forgiveness? Among people who understood the sacrifice of animals and offerings of incense to their gods but had no concept of living a life of personal sacrifice, a life of obedience and holiness before God?

How would Jesus' disciples, and — more importantly — *their* disciples, remain faithful to God in the environment of Asia Minor? How would the daily lives of new disciples change when they decided to follow Jesus? How would their neighbors, coworkers, and local officials react when they began living a radically different lifestyle? What price would the new disciples of Jesus pay? What would attract others to follow their lead? Would the fledgling community of Jesus be able to make disciples?

Although Jesus' disciples didn't have answers to these questions, they left behind the security and comfort of the small, rural villages of Galilee. They went out to tell the news of the kingdom of heaven and to make disciples in the bustling, sophisticated culture of the Roman world. When they did, the growth of the Christian faith exploded in large cities such as Ephesus, Pergamum, and Sardis as well as in smaller towns such as Priene and Miletus. Within a century, Christianity had swept across the world and culture of Asia Minor.

Today, among the ruins of the ancient seaport of Priene, we'll consider how those early Christian believers lived. Priene is not mentioned in the Bible, and we have no evidence that any of Jesus' disciples actually visited or taught there. But we do know that soon after the good news of Jesus arrived in Asia Minor, a vibrant Christian community existed there. We also know that Jesus' disciples were in the general area. Paul spent time in Miletus, which is visible across the valley from Priene, and Paul and John as well as other disciples lived in Ephesus, which was just over the mountains from Priene.

Let's see if we can discover where the new believers in Priene and other communities throughout Asia Minor found the faith and commitment to remain true to their Rabbi. To live out their faith was to stand against their culture, and new believers often gave up all social, economic, and political advantages. Sometimes they were viewed with suspicion because their new faith was thought to offend the gods. Despite these hardships, they had something their world lacked: a community of people who obeyed and loved God and who loved one another. As they expressed the love of God in word and deed, they made a tremendous impact on the world around them.

opening Thoughts (4 minutes)

The Very Words of God

They devoted themselves to the apostles' teaching and to the fellowship, to the breaking of bread and to prayer. Everyone was filled with awe, and many wonders and miraculous signs were done by

the apostles. . . . And the Lord added to their number daily those who
were being saved.

                                                                    Acts 2:42 – 43, 47

Think About It

What is it like when you move to a place you have never lived before and the way you think, what you like to talk about, the things you hold dear, and how you live life doesn't fit in with people around you? How do you create a place for yourself and find people who are like you?

DVD Notes (23 minutes)

The message of Jesus goes to Priene

The *agora*

The *bouleuterion*

What it meant to follow Jesus

Communities of worship

DVD Highlights (4 minutes)

1. How religious were the people of Priene, and in what ways did they practice their beliefs in everyday life?

   Why was it so important for them to be faithful to their gods?

2. Did you realize that the early Christians faced exclusion from all of the major institutions of their world—commercial (the marketplace), political (bouleuterion), religious (worship of the city's gods), and cultural (such as sources of water, fire, and food)—unless they were willing to publicly affirm the authority of pagan gods? What kind of an impact would being excluded have made on their daily lives?

3. What did Christian believers bring to the social order that Greek and Roman society had never seen before, and how did it affect the established social order?

Profile of a City:
Priene

The acropolis and lower city of Priene at the base of the cliff would have been visible from the sea during ancient times.

- Founded by Greeks about 1000 BC; became part of the Roman Empire in 167 BC.
- Originally was a seaport where the Meander River Valley opened to the sea; now is about ten miles inland.
- Located about forty miles from Ephesus, twenty-five miles from Miletus (see map on page 93).
- Was a typical, mid-sized Greek-Roman city with about thirty thousand to forty thousand inhabitants.
- The main part of the city was built on a plateau at the foot of a ridge of the Samsun Mountains. It was laid out in city blocks, with paved streets and running water brought by aqueduct from a mountain spring.
- Was prosperous and religious; its theater held about seven thousand people and is one of the best-preserved Hellenistic theaters in the world.
- Had Jewish and very early Christian inhabitants.

The lower city of Priene taken from the acropolis above.
The Aegean Sea used to come to the edge of the higher ground
where the fields, modern roads, and olive grove are today. The Athena
temple is the large structure with several erect columns (right circle).
The remains of the theater are highlighted in the left circle.

small group Bible Discovery and Discussion (18 minutes)

The Fire of God's Presence

The blessing and presence of the gods, as represented by the fire of the goddess Hestia in the town hall, was a priceless treasure to the citizens of Priene. They believed the fire washed away all of their offenses against the gods and ensured that the gods would continue to bless the city. The fire of God was important to the followers of Jesus too, but in an entirely different way.

The power of Jesus' disciples came from the real presence of God whose Spirit appeared at Pentecost in the symbol of fire and lived within them! The people of Priene who saw the disciples' unity, love, and commitment to the Scriptures experienced God's presence far more powerfully than in their own *prytaneion* (town hall). And many of them believed! Let's examine the "fire" of God that lived within the early believers who became God's presence in a pagan world.

For Greater Understanding...

Everyone in Priene knew where the divine presence was—in the prytaneion, where they believed the goddess Hestia's fire from Mount Olympus, brought to their city from Greece, burned continually on the sacred hearth. When people brought fire from Hestia's sacred hearth to their home hearth, they believed they were bringing the divine presence into their own homes.

If the fire in their home went out, they would immediately get fire from the prytaneion to restore the divine presence in their home. If the fire in the prytaneion went out, it was considered a disaster, and required a delegation from the city to travel to Greece and bring the fire back to rekindle the hearth of Hestia.

In the minds of the people of Priene, the fire in the sacred hearth was essential to their spiritual, economic, and physical well-being; thus the prytaneion was the religious and political heart of the community. The clerk of the prytaneion was responsible to recognize the presence of the gods in the city; to see that all the gods of the city were properly honored so they would not bring disaster; and most importantly, to keep Hestia's fire burning on the sacred hearth.

---

1. In each of the following instances, how did God reveal his presence? How did God's people respond?

   a. Exodus 3:1–6

   b. Exodus 19:16–19; 20:18–21

c.   1 Kings 18:22–24, 36–39

2. The Tent of Meeting and later the temple in Jerusalem were the
    places God had said he would live in the midst of his people.
    How did God make his presence known when these places of
    worship were dedicated to him? (See Leviticus 9:5–6, 22–24;
    2 Chronicles 7:1–4.)

3. What did the prophet Joel and John the Baptist predict regarding
    God's Spirit and how it would be represented? (See Joel 2:28–30;
    Matthew 3:11.)

4. Read Acts 2:1–4 and note what God did on the day of Pentecost
    as Jesus' disciples gathered in or near the temple.

    a. What happened? What did people see?

    b. What did the fire represent to the Jews? Where would they
        have thought it came from?

    c. On whom did God's presence rest? Where would God's presence—his "fire"—be from that day forward?

5. Once followers of Jesus arrived in Priene, where in the city would a person find God's true presence—his genuine fire?

In what ways do you think the new followers of Jesus in Priene realized this? How do you think they responded to the Pentecost story when they first heard it?

6. Every culture has its prytaneion—the beings, places, things, or ideas that people believe will keep their lives in order and avert disaster. With what do the people you know seek to keep their "hearth" lit? Where do they search for the "fire" they need?

Where is the *real* prytaneion in your community?

faith Lesson (5 minutes)

1. In Galatians 5:16–25, Paul writes about living by the Spirit of God.

    a. What happens when God's people live by the fire of his presence?

    b. Are you and your fellow believers seen as the presence of God in your community? Why or why not?

    c. In what ways do people who are not believers recognize God's presence when they come in contact with you? How can you know if they have seen God's presence in you?

2. Name a couple of specific ways you would like the Spirit of God, as it is visible in your life, to affect your community, your workplace, or your neighborhood.

closing (1 minute)

Pray together, asking God to fan the fire of his presence within you, so that your life will reveal Jesus to those around you.

Memorize

Don't you know that you yourselves are God's temple and that God's Spirit lives in you? If anyone destroys God's temple, God will destroy him; for God's temple is sacred, and you are that temple.

1 Corinthians 3:16–17

walking with the rabbi day by day

In-Depth Personal Study Sessions

day one/god prepared a world to receive his message!

The Very Words of God

Then he said to his disciples, "The harvest is plentiful but the workers are few. Ask the Lord of the harvest, therefore, to send out workers into his harvest field."

Matthew 9:37–38

Bible Discovery

Making Disciples in Asia Minor

The people of Asia Minor didn't need more gods. They were happy and prosperous enough with their own gods. They were confident of eternal life, had no sense of sin, and felt no need for forgiveness. Yet when the early Christians brought the message of the kingdom of God and lived that message in the midst of a pagan world, the awesome power of God turned that world upside down. People flocked to the community of Jesus. The more we know about the world of Asia Minor, the more clearly we understand God's call to live radically Christian lives.

Data File

Asia Minor (southwestern Turkey today) was one of the most heavily populated and wealthy provinces of the entire Roman Empire. The geography of the area is characterized by mountain ranges and wide river valleys that run perpendicular to the sea. These river valleys have fertile soil and allow moisture-laden air

---

from the sea to penetrate inland and produce abundant rain. In ancient times (as is true today) the area was famous for its vineyards, fruit trees, and other agricultural produce. Not only that, the coast provided many natural inlets that made excellent harbors, and the river valleys provided easy access routes from the coast to the interior.

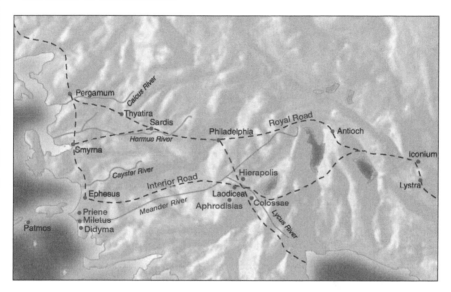

Trade routes of Asia Minor

Asia Minor is where East meets West. The center of the Roman Empire was in the West, but the goods it demanded came from the East and the fertile farms of Asia Minor. Major roads passed through the region from harbors on the Mediterranean and Aegean to the great civilizations of the East (such as Babylon) and South (the land route to Egypt through Israel). Commerce moved continually through the valleys and over the mountain passes. Large cities developed near harbors and along trade routes. Huge numbers of people from all over the world traveled through the region. Asia Minor became the crossroads of the Roman world. To be a witness for Jesus in Asia Minor was truly to be a witness to the world.

1. Somehow the early believers knew that Asia Minor was a strategic location to fulfill the Messiah's mandate. We don't know every disciple of Jesus who went to Asia Minor, but Scripture reveals several. (Historical records add to this list.)

   a. In which regions and cities of Asia did Paul teach? (See Acts 13–14; 16:1–10; 18:18–20:28.)

   b. What was the result of Paul's long-term teaching in Ephesus? (See Acts 19:10.)

   c. Which groups of believers did Peter write to in Asia Minor? What was his message to them? In what ways do you see Peter following the discipleship model Jesus had taught? (See 1 Peter 1:1–16.)

   d. To which believers did the apostle John write in the book of Revelation? In what ways was he being a disciple making disciples? (See Revelation 1:4–6; 1:9–3:22.)

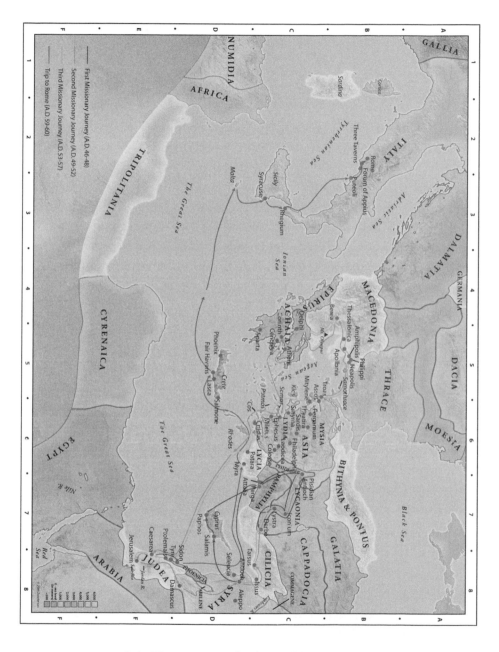

**Asia Minor was a major focus of the ministries
of Paul, Peter, John, and others.**

It's Amazing!
God Prepared the Way!

Far more than simply location and geography made Asia Minor the perfect place for Jesus' disciples to share the message of the kingdom of God with the world. God had been working for centuries to prepare this part of the world to receive his message.

The Greeks had colonized Asia Minor by 1200 BC, and when Alexander the Great liberated it from the Persians in the late fourth century BC, the Greek culture and language gained new vitality there. Heavy trade traffic through the region further strengthened the use of Greek as the common language, which later played a vital role in the rapid spread of Christianity.

The Persians conquered Asia Minor in 546 BC, after which the Jewish population grew rapidly. Some Jews came as slaves after the Assyrians destroyed the northern tribes. Isaiah refers to Jewish exiles in the lands of Asia Minor (Isaiah 66:19), and Obadiah records that exiles from Jerusalem were in Sepharad (Obadiah 13:20), which is believed to be Sardis. Many of these Jews retained their faith in the God of their fathers and made regular pilgrimages to Jerusalem (see Acts 2:9 – 10).

One of the Seleucid kings, Antiochus III, imported two thousand Jewish families from Babylon to Asia Minor. These Jews were known for their devotion to God that resulted in loyalty, honesty, and hard work. They formed prosperous communities in several key cities and for the most part were highly respected. Many of these Jews worshiped in their local synagogues and attended festivals in Jerusalem. When God sent his Spirit to the disciples in Jerusalem on Pentecost, some Jews who witnessed that event returned home to Asia Minor to spread the good news. When Paul and other early missionaries began teaching in Asia Minor, they first went to the synagogues of these faithful Jews.

In the midst of a notoriously immoral culture, the Jewish communities in Asia Minor also attracted Gentile followers.

These Gentiles, sometimes called "God fearers," adopted Jewish practices such as Sabbath-keeping, festivals, and Torah study. Who would have predicted that faithful Jews and God-fearing Gentiles in Asia Minor would be the soil in which the new faith of the disciples would take root and bear great fruit?

Reflection

What do you learn from the amazing impact the early disciples of Jesus had on Asia Minor, the most pagan province of the Roman world?

How can today's followers of Jesus make a significant and positive impact on our culture, which is remarkably similar to that of Asia Minor in the first century?

What attracted the people of Asia Minor to the Christian faith? What attracts (and does not attract) people to the Christian faith today?

day two/culture clash in the marketplace

The Very Words of God

But just as he who called you is holy, so be holy in all you do; for it is written: "Be holy, because I am holy."

1 Peter 1:15–16

Bible Discovery

Standing Against the Culture

Galilee and Asia Minor were similar in that virtually everything in both cultures had some religious significance. But the manifestation of religious priorities in daily life was vastly different. Daily life for Jews in Galilee centered on obediently following God in every way possible. Daily life in Asia Minor centered on pleasing the gods to win their favor and ensure personal success, which allowed them to indulge in every pleasure the gods offered. How did the early Christians live out their faith when their lifestyle priorities opposed those of their culture?

Data File

Followers of Christ and the Agora

The focal point of an ancient Greek or Roman city's economic, cultural, political, and religious life was usually found in the *agora*, or central marketplace. The agora was part mall, part flea market, and part public square. It was usually a large, rectangular space surrounded by a colonnade. Permanent shops were located under the roof of the colonnade, and the open area would be crowded with the stalls of farmers and merchants who had come to sell their wares.

In addition to being the center of commerce, the agora was the center of public life. Between transactions, people in the agora chatted about business, trends, politics, and religion. The bouleuterion and prytaneion (the buildings of local government) were usually adjacent to the agora, so it was a place where local officials often gathered. Public fountains in the agora served the shopkeepers as well as those who could not afford to have running water in their homes. Statues to the city's gods, political figures, and athletes could be found in the agora as well.

The Priene agora

One of the difficulties for the early Christians was that an altar or shrine to the primary god(s) of the city also stood in the agora. (Priene's agora honored Zeus and Athena, for example.) Before selling goods in the agora, a merchant would honor the city's god(s) by "offering" or "dedicating" those goods to the god(s). Meat sold in the agora had either been "offered" in this way or portions had actually been sacrificed in the god's temple and brought to the agora for sale.

The disciples of Jesus naturally faced serious economic consequences if they refused to honor the gods in the agora. Because all the meat available had either been sacrificed or "offered" to pagan gods, they had to decide whether or not to eat it. So the questions, *Should we eat this meat? Should we buy these goods offered to other gods? How will we sell our products if we won't honor the god(s) of the agora?* were no trivial matter for those who followed the Rabbi. These often were questions of life and death.

One area in which the values of early Christians opposed those of the culture at large was in the making, buying, and selling of goods. In Asia Minor, every trade—from potters to farmers to sandal makers—had a guild, and every tradesperson belonged to that guild. Each guild had a god, and guild members celebrated and sacrificed to that god. In addition, everyone who had products to sell had to "dedicate" or "devote" those goods to the honor of the god(s) of the city.

1. Read 1 Corinthians 8:4–13; 10:25–29 and Acts 15:19–29.

    a. What problems did the early believers face (in Greece as well as in Asia Minor) in relationship to idol worship? How big a problem was this?

    b. As you read the solutions Paul and the leaders in Jerusalem presented, what do you notice about the role of community in practicing obedience and in the life of the early church?

    c. Do you think Paul's solution to the problem of eating meat sacrificed to idols applied to other goods as well? Why or why not?

2. Sacrifices and offerings made in obedience to God were nothing
    new to the Jews or early Christians.

    a. What did the Israelites do in obedience to God? (See Leviti-
        cus 1–2; 27:30–32.)

    b. What are believers to offer in obedience to God? (See Romans
        6:11–14; 12:1–2.)

    c. What do we indicate if we "offer" ourselves to someone or
        something other than God?

Profile of the Guilds

Craftsmen and farmers belonged to trade guilds that were
licensed by Roman authorities. The guilds provided standards for
the production and marketing of goods but were primarily centers of social and religious life. Entire families belonged to their
respective guilds, and guild activities shaped their lives. Members
of a particular guild often lived in a common area of a city and
sold their goods together in the agora. Each guild had a patron
god or goddess, and most guild activities focused on honoring and
worshiping that deity to ensure the guild's economic success.

Guild activities are well documented (the rules can still be
found on some ancient temple walls). The celebrations often
were held in the temple of the guild's patron deity and were
notoriously immoral. The guild feast began with animal sacrifices (sometimes by strangulation) at the temple altar, followed
by consumption of the meat (sometimes raw). Guests with the
highest status received the best places, were served before others,

and received the best food and wine. The slaves and lower-status members often went hungry because there was no food left for them. A drinking party followed. The women would leave, but they would be replaced by male (often young boys) and female companions who provided sexual favors for guild members.

If a guild existed for the products you made or sold, you were socially and/or officially pressured to join that guild. If you refused to join, the *agoranomos* (agora director) might not let you into the agora. Other guild members would prevent you from receiving raw materials or the benefit of their advertising. People in the community would refuse to buy your merchandise out of fear that they would offend the god(s) of the guild or the city. It probably was not unusual for a new believer who refused to participate in a guild to lose income and occupation.

3. Based on 1 Corinthians 10:6–22; Acts 15:19–22, 29; and Revelation 2:20–22, what kinds of problems did the early church face in connection with guild feasts, and how did the apostles address them?

4. Read John 17:16–19 and 1 Corinthians 1:2; 6:19–20.

   a. What did Jesus pray for his followers? How important was it for the believers in Priene, Corinth, and other cities throughout the Roman Empire to be holy and pure? Why?

   b. In what ways do you think the early believers could be holy and pure in the midst of the agora, in the environment of guilds?

Did You Know?

Tentmaking was an excellent trade for someone who traveled as much as Paul. The few tools required (awl, knife, needles, and thread) could be carried easily, and raw materials were available nearly everywhere. The canvas, linen, and leather coverings a tentmaker produced were needed for army tents, for sails, and for awnings. It is possible that Paul's move to Corinth coincided with the AD 51 Isthmian Olympic Games, during which there would have been great demand for tentmaking (Acts 18:1–3).

As a tentmaker, Paul could earn a living in places such as the agora where he could talk with people about the God of the Hebrews and his Messiah Son, Jesus. Because Paul was a Jew, and Jews were granted certain exemptions from honoring other gods, it is likely that Paul was not required to offer incense to the gods of the agora. The work was very hard, and tentmakers developed strong, calloused hands. When working with leather, for example, the stitch was set with a sudden pull using both hands. This may explain Paul's apparent difficulty in writing (Galatians 6:11).

Fact File

The Agoranomos

The *agoranomos*, or inspector of market transactions in the agora, was very powerful. Consider some of his responsibilities:

- Determined the accuracy of weights and measures.
- Assigned appropriate space to each merchant.
- Controlled prices.
- Determined whether specific goods had been produced by members of that trade guild in good standing and therefore produced in devotion to the god of the guild.

- Ensured that goods were devoted to the gods represented in his particular agora.
- Could prevent Jesus' disciples from entering the agora if they did not recognize its god(s) or participate in the guilds.

Reflection

John, the author of Revelation, is traditionally believed to have lived in Ephesus, one of the largest cities in the ancient world. Ephesus was such a busy seaport that the city had two agoras—one primarily for the city and its residents and another for commercial business near the harbor. Imagine what his readers thought when they read the following prophecy:

The merchants of the earth will weep and mourn over her because no one buys their cargoes any more—cargoes of gold, silver, precious stones and pearls; fine linen, purple, silk and scarlet cloth; every sort of citron wood, and articles of every kind made of ivory, costly wood, bronze, iron and marble; cargoes of cinnamon and spice, of incense, myrrh and frankincense, of wine and olive oil, of fine flour and wheat; cattle and sheep; horses and carriages; and bodies and souls of men.

They will say, "The fruit you longed for is gone from you. All your riches and splendor have vanished, never to be recovered." The merchants who sold these things and gained their wealth from her will stand far off, terrified at her torment. They will weep and mourn.

Revelation 18:11–15

Think about the importance of the "agora" in your life. Think not only of the fine and beautiful things, but the essentials of life. As a follower of Christ, how do you put it all in perspective?

What would you do if your faith in Jesus meant that you could not participate in the working world of your culture, causing you to lose income, status, etc.?

On the other hand, what opportunities are there in the agora of today to make disciples?

How much of the phenomenal growth of the early church in Priene and similar places might have been due to the believers' willingness to obey God even if it cost them greatly? How did the early believers manage to make these sacrifices? What resulted from their sacrifices, and what do we learn from them?

Day Three/excluded from political power

The Very Words of God

You must be on your guard. You will be handed over to the local councils and flogged in the synagogues. On account of me you will stand before governors and kings as witnesses to them.

Mark 13:9

Bible Discovery

Powerless Yet Influential

From the DVD, we gained insight into the bouleuterion of Priene and why disciples of Jesus would be excluded from that important leadership council. It was not uncommon for Jesus and his disciples to face opposition from established authorities. Yet even the most powerful leaders were powerless to silence the disciples or diminish the power of their message.

1. What had Jesus warned his disciples concerning their relationship with unbelievers and their governments? In what way had this prepared the disciples, especially those who had Zealot tendencies, for what was ahead? (See Luke 12:11 – 12; John 15:18 – 25.)

2. Read Jeremiah 27:5 – 7 and Isaiah 44:24 – 28.

    a. What do these passages reveal about the authorities — yes, even pagan authorities — that are in place in this world?

    b. We know that Jesus' disciples knew the Hebrew text. How do you think knowing these truths encouraged them when existing authorities threatened them?

    c. Could the authorities and the power they used to threaten the disciples ever deter the message of the kingdom of God? Why or why not?

3. Who has the ultimate authority in all things and why? (See Matthew 28:18; John 17:1–2; Colossians 1:15–20.)

4. Why were the disciples willing to submit themselves to existing earthly authorities? What was their purpose in doing so? (See Romans 13:1–7; Titus 3:1–2; 1 Peter 2:13–15.)

5. Scripture records a number of accounts of early believers in conflict with existing authorities. Read Acts 4:1–21; 16:16–40; 17:16–34.

    a. In each of these situations, what kind of influence did the believers lack, and what kind of influence did they have?

    b. What did the believers' influence accomplish in terms of teaching the message of the kingdom of God?

Data File

The Bouleuterion

The disciples of Jesus took their message to a world under Rome's authority, but daily life was governed on the local level as long as it did not oppose Rome. Cities, towns, and villages were democracies ruled by a town council (*boule*, Greek) that met in the *bouleuterion*, or council house. Elected by citizens, this influential council passed laws concerning local life, much as a city council does today. So the local bouleuterion was the center of political influence in the Roman world.

Virtually all of ancient Roman life was religious, and politics was no exception. In the bouleuterion of Priene, for example, stands a cube-shaped altar with a carving of a god on each of four sides. Although the altar is damaged, the gods are believed to be Hermes, Heracles, Apollo, and Aesclepius. A fire of coals glowed on the top of the altar whenever the council met, and each member was required to place incense on that altar to honor the gods.

This practice obviously created a problem for Christians who would not recognize the authority of other gods. What ruling council would allow members whose refusal to honor the gods could threaten the very security of the town or city? For those of us who live in a democracy where the Christian faith is a legal religion, it is hard to imagine the impact that following Jesus had on one's opportunity to participate in the political arena.

Reflection

In what ways and to what degree do you think the early believers — those who lived in Priene, for example — were intimidated by the economic, social, and political power of city officials and of the Roman Empire?

In what ways were you surprised that Christianity spread so rapidly from people who had virtually no economic or political power?

Read Ephesians 6:10–20. What does Paul command? Why?

Make a list of the armor of God. How does this armor give you courage and commitment to stand firm against authorities that would silence the message of the kingdom of heaven?

Pray that you and your faith community will use the armor necessary to stand firm against the power of evil and the evil one—whether in politics, economics, or any other sphere of life.

Day four/communities of faith

The Very Words of God

"My prayer is not for them alone. I pray also for those who will believe in me through their message, that all of them may be one, Father, just as you are in me and I am in you. May they also be in us so that the world may believe that you have sent me. I have given them the glory that you gave me, that they may be one as we are one: I in them and you in me. May they be brought to complete unity to let the world know that you sent me and have loved them even as you have loved me."

John 17:20–23

Bible Discovery

God Accomplishes His Work in Community

Throughout Scripture we see God accomplishing his work with individuals in the context of community. Individual actions affected the community; God's work within the community affected individuals; and the community affected the world around it. So it wasn't just great preaching and teaching that caused the Christian faith to explode onto the scene in Asia Minor. It was also the Christian commitment to live in obedience to God in community, as practiced in hundreds of small house churches scattered across the Roman Empire.

The "house synagogue" in Priene

1. Where did Jesus live with his disciples when they were training to become like him? How do you think this housing situation affected the disciples' obedience to the Rabbi's teaching? Why? (See Matthew 13:1, 36; Mark 1:29–36; 2:1–2; 10:10.)

2. Where did Jesus tell his disciples to live when he sent them out to preach the kingdom of God? What impact might this have had on their future ministry? (See Luke 9:1–6.)

3. In what kinds of places did Paul meet people and teach them? What does this tell you about his passion to make disciples? (See Acts 16:13–15, 27–34, 40; 17:10–12, 16–17; 18:7–8, 18–19; 20:20.)

Did You Know?

The Bible and archaeological finds reveal that church buildings did not exist until the early third century. The early Christian movement lacked major resources, so believers simply met and worshiped in their homes—much like the worship in house synagogues of the time.

---

4. What evidence do we have that the discipleship model Jesus used to teach and train his disciples was alive and well in the early churches? How effective was this model in teaching new believers and making disciples? (See 1 Corinthians 4:16–17; Philemon 1–2; 1 Thessalonians 1:4–10.)

5. What kind of language did Jesus' disciples and the early Christian believers use to describe themselves and their relationship to one another? What does this tell us about the early community of Jesus? In what ways do their descriptions differ from how Christians today describe our faith communities? (See Acts 16:15; Ephesians 2:19–20; Philippians 4:21–22; 1 Timothy 3:14–15.)

6. What kinds of behavior toward one another characterized the early church? What does this reveal about the nature of the early church? (See Galatians 2:9; 6:10; Romans 16:16; 1 Corinthians 16:19–20; 1 Peter 3:8.)

Think About It

God wants the world to know who he is by the way his disciples live in community.

Ray Vander Laan

Reflection

What in their Galilean roots led the early Christians to develop house-based churches where members had everything in common and shared with others in need?

To what extent and in what ways do you think "house churches" shaped the early believing community and contributed to the spread of the gospel?

In what way(s) does the local church body as we know it today enhance or hinder the process of disciple making?

Which characteristics of the early church might we desire to reclaim? Why?

Do you think a person can become a true disciple as Jesus intended apart from a "household" or community where one learns obedience to Jesus? Why or why not? How willing are you to become a devoted part of a discipling community?

For Greater Understanding
What Made the Early Christian Faith So Attractive?

- God blessed the message and those who received it.
- People followed Jesus because God blessed the great preaching and teaching of Paul, Peter, John, and many others.
- People were attracted to the message because their broken and immoral society was empty and unsatisfying. They saw among the believers love and unity for one another and a love for those around them.
- The Greco-Roman world emphasized the individual at the expense of the group; competition reigned supreme; and class distinctions were inviolable. In contrast, the early church was a community modeled after the extended family. It had few class distinctions, and its members graciously cared for one another and strangers who desired to join them.

Memorize

The churches in the province of Asia send you greetings. Aquila and Priscilla greet you warmly in the Lord, and so does the church that meets at their house. All the brothers here send you greetings. Greet one another with a holy kiss.

1 Corinthians 16:19–20

Day five/Love: Living evidence of the presence of god

The Very Words of God

You are no longer foreigners and aliens, but fellow citizens with God's people and members of God's household, built on the foundation of the apostles and prophets, with Christ Jesus himself as the chief cornerstone. In him the whole building is joined together and rises to become a holy temple in the Lord.

Ephesians 2:19–21

Bible Discovery

Love Demonstrates God's Presence

Jesus emphasized that his disciples would demonstrate the "fire of God" within them through love and unity. Read each of the following passages, which encourage every disciple to love as Jesus loved. Consider the many ways love demonstrates God's presence in our lives. Write down as many specific examples as you see in these passages.

1. Forgive each other: 2 Corinthians 2:5–11; Colossians 3:13.

2. Love each other: Ephesians 5:1–2; 1 John 4:7–12.

3. Share with those in need: 1 John 3:16–20; Romans 12:13; Ephesians 4:28; 1 Timothy 6:18; Hebrews 13:1–3, 16.

4. Show compassion: Ephesians 4:32.

5. Do not bring lawsuits or publicly defame Jesus and his followers: 1 Corinthians 6:1–8.

6. Show tolerance; avoid anger, favoritism, and gossip; promote peace: James 1:19–21, 26; 2:1–9; 3:3–6, 17–18.

7. Don't seek revenge: Romans 12:9–21.

8. Show hospitality: Matthew 25:35–36; 1 Peter 4:8–9.

9. Accept one another's differences: Romans 14:1–21; 15:1–7.

10. Pray for one another, confess sin to each other: James 5:13–20.

11. Have unity: Galatians 3:26–28.

Reflection

To what extent are love and unity still proving that Jesus' message and our faith are genuine? Explain your answer.

In what way(s) have Christian communities you are familiar with expressed their love for God, for one another, and others? In what ways are expressions of love lacking in your faith community?

Pray for the love and unity of the church of Jesus and your own community of faith. Take the time to consider how the demonstrations of love and unity you discovered in the Scriptures can be exhibited in your world. Pray that each will be a reality in your life and the life of your faith community.

Session 4

Living Stones

Jesus' disciples knew the significance of the living God's presence among them. Three times each year they had walked from their homes in Galilee to Jerusalem. With thousands of God-fearing Jews from all of Israel and the surrounding nations, they had gathered in awe before the great temple in which the presence of almighty God resided. Generations earlier, near where Abraham had expected to sacrifice his beloved Isaac, King David purchased land for a temple to God that his son, Solomon, later built. When that temple was dedicated, God lived in it in a dramatic way. God finally had a magnificent building in which to live in the midst of his people!

Later, because of Israel's unfaithfulness, God permitted his temple to be destroyed. Zerubbabel began rebuilding it, then Herod renovated it in great splendor. God still lived in that temple in the midst of his people. Imagine the joy and awe that Jesus, his disciples, and other Jews felt in God's presence—the same joy their ancestors had shared. Even after Jesus ascended to heaven, his disciples continued to join the community of God's people in celebrating God's presence in his temple.

But Pentecost initiated a pivotal change. Jesus had commissioned his disciples to "go and make disciples of all nations." They were to leave the temple, leave the community of God's people, and take God's presence with them to people who had never seen the temple in Jerusalem and did not know the living God of Israel. So the disciples went out to people who had their own temples—spectacular structures built to honor a host of pagan deities. These people never imagined they needed news of another god. Yet they responded in droves when the disciples, armed with love and equipped with the presence of God, took the message of his kingdom to them.

How did Jesus' inner circle of disciples and the disciples they made follow the Rabbi when they were surrounded by pagan temples that declared the greatness and glory of other gods? Would Jesus' disciples continue to point people to the temple, or "house of the Lord," in Jerusalem? How would the destruction of the temple in AD 70, shortly after the disciples reached Asia Minor, affect God's presence in their lives? How would they ever convince the people of Asia Minor that they served a mighty God when they didn't have a building to show how great and powerful he was or to demonstrate how much they honored him?

As we'll see, God did not abandon his people after his temple in Jerusalem was destroyed. In fact, he had already set into motion an amazing plan to make known his presence in the world in an even more personal and dramatic way. God's plan for revealing his presence would not only meet the deepest needs of Jesus' disciples, but would communicate volumes to people who worshiped pagan deities in man-made temples of stone.

opening Thoughts (4 minutes)

The Very Words of God

Consequently, you are no longer foreigners and aliens, but fellow citizens with God's people and members of God's household, built on the foundation of the apostles and prophets, with Christ Jesus himself as the chief cornerstone. In him the whole building is joined together and rises to become a holy temple in the Lord. And in him you too are being built together to become a dwelling in which God lives by his Spirit.

Ephesians 2:19–22

Think About It

We all know a temple is a place dedicated to the worship of a deity. But what else is a temple? What makes a temple special? Why do people build them? What does a temple represent to the worshipers and to people outside the worshiping community?

DVD Notes (21 minutes)

Goddest
↑
Athena, pride of Priene (Turkey) - Temple

→ From the God of heaven

- Water from God / miracle

✱ we are the temple of God
God dwells w/in

The temple, monument to greatness

Where is God's temple?   We are the temple

The "living stones" of God's temple

The power of God's love

- We are design to where we should
fit in God's will

- love one another as I loved you

DVD Highlights (4 minutes)

1. What impressed you regarding the significance of the Athena temple to the people, culture, and status of Priene?

2. In our culture, we tend to take such things as running water for granted. What message did the fountain of water near the Athena temple in Priene communicate to the people?

   In what ways would your perceptions of life and God change if you were to recognize and thank God for every little gift that makes your life possible?

3. In ancient times, a temple was an important expression of the greatness of a god. It took decades, sometimes centuries, to build a temple appropriate for a great god. How does understanding the importance of a temple built by human hands help you to understand how God views you as a "living stone" being built into the temple in which he lives?

Data File
The Athena Temple, the Pride of Priene

One of the finest architects of the ancient world, Pythias, designed the temple of Athena in Priene. The one-hundred-by-fifty-five-foot structure stood more than seventy feet high! It was surrounded by a single row of thirty, fluted, white marble columns, each of which was forty-five feet tall and more than six feet in diameter. Built on the highest point within the city of Priene, the temple building could be seen for miles to the east, south, and west. The beauty, grace, size, and engineering of this great temple, on which construction began in the fourth century BC, served as a pattern for other temples for centuries. After biblical times, the temple was destroyed by an earthquake.

The Athena temple in Priene

The *temenos*, the larger sacred enclosure surrounding the temple building, was spectacular as well. This area, about 300 by 175 feet in size, was paved with marble quarried in local mountains. The large stones used in the outer supporting walls were cut with such precision that no mortar was needed.

Within the temenos, in the open area in front of the temple, stood a great altar (forty-five feet long and twenty-two feet wide). The walls of the altar featured carved marble reliefs of robed female figures slightly smaller than life size. These pieces are some of the finest examples of sculpture ever found from the ancient world. Along the length of the south side of the temenos was a *stoa*, or colonnaded building, with a long row of statues representing other gods, local heroes, or leading citizens.

Within the temple structure, a set of double wooden doors opened to reveal a twenty-one-foot-tall statue of Athena. The huge doors, likely covered with bronze, were about twenty-five feet tall and six feet wide and swung open on giant pins. The statue, a replica of the great statue of Athena by Pheidias that stood in the Parthenon, was probably covered with gold, bronze, ivory, and marble. Imagine the sight when the east-facing doors swung open in the morning and the sunlight reflected off the magnificent statue. Onlookers must have been dazzled by the greatness of the Athena of Priene. The scene certainly would have instilled awe and admiration for her.

Statue of the goddess Athena

small Group Bible Discovery and Discussion (20 minutes)

Where Is God's Temple?

Temples were everywhere in Asia Minor. You couldn't miss them. They often were built on hilltops, and some of them were huge. Many of them were masterful works of art and engineering crafted by the finest stonecutters and sculptors.

Not only were the ancient temples visual focal points, they were cultural focal points as well. A temple was the dwelling place of a deity that provided the necessities of life — water, food, health, safety. It was central to many of a city's festivals and celebrations. And the connection between the temple and the guilds made it central to the economy. So what was it like for disciples of Jesus in Asia Minor to follow a God who didn't have a temple like other gods?

1. Read Acts 17:22–29. What key questions regarding the nature of his God did Paul explain to the men of Athens?

    Why would these have been important to his audience there as well as in Asia Minor?

    What further questions do you think Paul's explanation might have prompted?

2. Scripture provides several images of God's temple in 1 Corinthians 3:16–17; 6:19–20 and Ephesians 2:19–22. Read these passages and try to understand them as if you were a resident of Corinth, Ephesus, or any other first-century Roman city. Then answer the following questions:

    a. Of what is God's temple made? Is it complete? Explain your answer.

    b. What lives in God's temple? What makes it sacred?

    c. How highly does God value his temple? What impact should this have on how we value it?

3. See Hebrews 3:3–6. Who is building God's temple (or house)?

What does this mean for every believer?

4. In what ways is it easy and/or difficult for you to comprehend and envision the idea of God building a temple of people who follow him?

5. In the cities of Asia Minor, a temple or monument to a god was nearly always in view. How often during a day do you think the image of being God's temple crossed the early believers' minds and influenced their thoughts, words, and deeds?

6. What do you think the people of Priene thought about a god whose temple was not a stunning architectural creation but a loving community of people fully committed to Jesus and the Scriptures?

7. For nearly a thousand years, the God of Israel lived in a temple made by human hands. Why do you think God chose to live — to build his new temple — in the community of his disciples?

In what ways does a temple of people differ from a temple of stone in terms of its beauty, its permanence, its power, and its ability to influence the world around it?

Think About It

Imagine that you were an intensely devoted follower of Athena. You had participated in her festivals all your life (as had your family and almost everyone else you knew). Last month, through the witness of a follower of Jesus, you decided to turn your back on Athena and become a Jesus follower yourself, a worshiper of the God of the Jews.

- How might your family, friends, and neighbors respond to this dramatic change? How might these relationships change?
- What might they ask about your new faith?
- What might they say about your new perspective that Athena is a powerless figment of someone's imagination?
- What might you wonder about having a temple dedicated to Jesus? Why?

Faith Lesson (5 minutes)

1. To come face to face with the presence of God is always a powerful thing. Read 2 Chronicles 7:1–3 and note where God's glory lived. Then read Matthew 24:1; Mark 13:1; and Luke 21:5 and note how Jesus' disciples responded to the temple of God in Jerusalem. What does their response indicate?

2. Although the descent of God's presence on Mount Sinai, the dedication of the temple, and Pentecost are more overt, dramatic expressions, it would be a mistake to think that God's presence wasn't evident in other ways too. The Hebrew text reveals numerous instances of how God's presence within his people made an impact on the world around them. Several examples are highlighted in the following passages. Read each one and consider the ways nonbelievers responded to God's presence in his people.

    a. Genesis 41:37–40

    b. Exodus 18:1, 9–12

    c. Daniel 3:28–30; 6:19–28

3. Given the examples from question 2, how might nonbelievers respond to God's presence as it is revealed through the "living stones" of his people today? What specific evidence in a believer's life would cause a person to say, "Aha! There is God!" or "That person speaks for God!"?

closing (1 minute)

Read the following Scripture passage aloud. Then pray, asking God to use this session to help fashion you into a living stone that fits perfectly into the temple Jesus is building to display God's greatness to the world.

Memorize

Don't you know that you yourselves are God's temple and that God's Spirit lives in you? If anyone destroys God's temple, God will destroy him; for God's temple is sacred, and you are that temple.

1 Corinthians 3:16–17

walking with the rabbi day by day

In-Depth Personal Study Sessions

day one/building a temple for god

The Very Words of God

They devoted themselves to the apostles' teaching and to the fellowship, to the breaking of bread and to prayer. Everyone was filled with awe, and many wonders and miraculous signs were done by the apostles. All the believers were together and had everything in common. Selling their possessions and goods, they gave to anyone as he had need.... And the Lord added to their number daily those who were being saved.

Acts 2:42–45, 47

Bible Discovery

What Is the Purpose of a Temple?

In ancient times, people built temples to make a god's presence known in the community in a big way. A large or beautiful temple was one way to show off the greatness of the god. Another way to display a god's greatness was to generously provide for the people's needs by making available fresh water, food, clothing, and in some cases medical care and entertainment.

When Jesus' disciples began making disciples in Asia Minor, how would the people around them recognize the presence of God? How would people who expected glorious temples and free "stuff" see the God of the disciples? What would the community of believers who lacked a physical temple do to display God's greatness to their world? How would they demonstrate his compassion and concern for the needs of the people?

1. Of what is God's temple, sometimes called God's "spiritual house," comprised? What is its purpose, and how is that purpose fulfilled? (See 1 Peter 2: 4–5, 12.)

2. Read Acts 2:42–47, describing the early church in Jerusalem shortly after Pentecost.

   a. In what ways were these disciples being a temple to God and putting his presence on display?

   b. What parallels or similarities do you see between this temple to God and the Athena temple in Priene?

   c. What kind of an impact did the temple of disciples have on those who saw it?

3. During his ministry on earth, Jesus went out into the Decapolis, the Gentile world close to Galilee. (See Matthew 15:29–37.)

   a. What happened when the presence of God as displayed in the body of Jesus showed up? How did the people respond?

   b. What does this suggest about the impact that the body of Jesus—the temple of his Spirit—should have in today's world?

4. Read Matthew 25:31–46, where Jesus taught about God being on his throne in glory and discerning and judging the works of people.

   a. What do the "sheep" who follow Jesus do? In what ways do these actions display God's presence? How does God view these actions?

   b. In light of the benefits that some pagan temples provided for people, what do you think resulted when Jesus' disciples provided water, food, clothing, and other necessities in the name of God?

Reflection

Read the following passages and note what they reveal about the community of God and its responsibility to be the "temple" in whom God lives.

   a. Hebrews 13:1–3

   b. Leviticus 19:18, 34; 23:22

   c. Deuteronomy 10:17–19; 27:19

d. Romans 12:13

Think about what a temple built to display these things would communicate about God—in the world of Asia Minor and in your world. Describe what it would look like to display these things in your world today. Be specific.

What kind of a statement does your life make about the God you follow? In what ways do people see the presence of God when they see you? How do they respond to God when they interact with you?

The Truth of the Matter

Knowing theology and proclaiming the gospel are important. Jesus did both. He was the presence of God to everyone he met through his teaching and love. He taught using powerful words and such actions as providing bread for the hungry, touch for the untouchable leper, sympathy for the grieving, and acceptance of the unloved. He desires his disciples to be like him. We must be the loving presence of God—his temple—wherever we are.

Ray Vander Laan

Consider how you and your faith community can do a better job of fulfilling your purpose as God's temple in your community.

Day Two/The stones of god's temple

The Very Words of God

The stone the builders rejected has become the capstone; the LORD has done this, and it is marvelous in our eyes.

Psalm 118:22–23

Bible Discovery

Who Are the Stones of God's Temple?

Temples were everywhere in the ancient world—Egypt, Israel, Persia, Asia Minor, Macedonia (Greece), and Rome—and they were built almost entirely of stone. So the inspired writers of Scripture had opportunities to use rich, stone-related metaphors to describe God and his people. Jews (and many Gentiles) who were familiar with God's temple in Jerusalem, and even believers who were familiar with such temples as the one for Athena in Priene, clearly understood the meaning behind these metaphors. They could see what it meant to be a living stone fashioned for a specific place in God's temple. They grasped the idea of God and Jesus being the Rock. They immediately recognized the importance of Jesus, when he is described as the cornerstone. We, on the other hand, have to work a bit to understand these themes that were central to the faith of the early believers.

1. Several key passages will help you form a picture of who is being built into God's temple and how it all fits together. Read each passage on the following page, fill in the information requested (the first one has been done for you), then answer the questions that follow.

Scripture Text	The Stone (the Person/s)	The Part Built or Being Built
Ps. 118:22–23	The stone the builders rejected (Jesus)	The capstone
Isa. 28:16		
Isa. 33:5–6		
1 Cor. 3:11		
Eph. 2:19–20		
1 Peter 2:4–6		

a. Who is the foundation of the temple of the Holy Spirit, the cornerstone from which all the other stones are fitted?

b. Who is the capstone, the final stone that holds all the other stones together?

c. Who, then, were the stones of God's temple in Priene? Describe in your own words what that would have meant to you if you had been a believer there. How would you have thought of yourself? How would that realization have affected your daily life?

**The foundation wall for the temenos of the Athena temple in Priene.
Notice the precise cutting and placement of the stones. This wall was built
during the fourth century BC and survived the earthquakes
that toppled the temple structure above it.**

2. Which metaphor does Paul use to describe Jesus in 1 Corinthians 10:1 – 4? What does this passage say about the spiritual heritage of those who follow Jesus? What do we share with those who have gone before us?

3. According to Isaiah 51:1 – 2, from which rock are those who seek the Lord cut? Who else has come from that same quarry? What would that mean to you as a believer in Priene? What does it mean to you today?

Did You Know?

Isaiah wrote that each believer, each "living stone" (1 Peter 2:4–5) that God is using for his purposes, comes from the common quarry of God's people (Isaiah 51:1–2). Thus God continues to "quarry" stones from the rock of Abraham, Sarah, David, Ruth, and other faithful believers. Like those "living stones" that came before us, we are being shaped by God, the great stone cutter. Although each of us is a different stone cut for a unique purpose, we each have great value as part of his temple.

Reflection

The early disciples understood that God was building a magnificent temple to honor his greatness with the "stones" of the lives of those who followed him faithfully. Living in a world surrounded by temples to many gods, the early disciples must have had dozens of reminders every day of who they needed to be, of how they needed to live in order to be a "stone" in the temple that honored God.

What in your world reminds you of how God wants to use you in his plans?

Paul taught the Corinthians how important it was for them to be aware of what they were building with their lives and why. Read 1 Corinthians 3:10–17 several times and consider the foundation on which you are building your life.

What kind of building stone are you?

In what ways is the quality of your effort worthy of God's temple? In what ways is it unworthy?

In what ways do you live as if you are part of God's temple in whom his Spirit lives?

What does it mean to you that God would rather live in you and have you show off his presence to the world than to live in the most beautiful temple in the world?

Day Three/You Are a Living Stone!

The Very Words of God

As you come to him, the living Stone — rejected by men but chosen by God and precious to him — you also, like living stones, are being built into a spiritual house to be a holy priesthood, offering spiritual sacrifices acceptable to God through Jesus Christ.

1 Peter 2:4–5

Bible Discovery

A Temple of Living Stones

Rock, a common sight in the Middle East, is often used as a metaphor in the Hebrew and Christian Scriptures. Jesus the Messiah, for example, is portrayed as the Rock. Rock is also a symbol for God and his faithfulness, so God's people used stones as monuments to God's faithfulness. The idea that God would refer to his people as living stones that he was building into a temple to display his faithfulness would not have seemed at all unusual to Jesus' disciples and the early believers.

1. Read the following Scriptures (see the chart below and on page 138). As you read each passage, write down the purpose for the stones and what they communicated at the time as well as in later generations:

Scripture	The purpose for the stones	What the stones communicated at the time	What the stones communicated to later generations
Gen. 35:1–3, 14–15			
Ex. 20:25			
Ex. 24:1–5			
Ex. 28:6–12			
Ex. 34:1, 27–28			
Josh. 3:14–4:9, 20–24			
Josh. 24:19–27			

1 Kings 5:15 – 18; 7:9 – 12			
1 Kings 18:30 – 38			

2. Think about what you have learned about temples and what they communicated to people during New Testament times. What similarities do you see between what a temple represents and what the living stones described above represent?

3. How do we know that the Spirit of God lives in each individual "living stone"? What does that make every believer? (See 1 Corinthians 6:19 – 20; Romans 8:9 – 11.)

4. Read 1 Corinthians 3:16; Ephesians 2:19 – 22; and 1 Peter 2:5.

   a. Of what is God's temple made?

   b. How many temples is God building?

   c. Why is it important that all of the stones be joined together? What can a temple of living stones accomplish that cannot be accomplished by individual living stones?

Reflection

As the early Christians realized that they were the living stones of God's house, what would that have meant to them? How would it have shaped their view of themselves and their community?

How does the truth of who we are as "living stones" affect your view of the people of God—including those who, in the world's eyes, seem to have little value?

Why did God command his people to set up stone (rock) memorials? What impact do you think those memorials had on people who passed by them later? As you have learned about these memorials, what have they caused you to remember, think about, or do?

Where might you place a memorial of stones or rocks to remind yourself of what God has done and is doing in your life or the life of someone you love? What would such a memorial commemorate? What impact would you like it to have on your life? What impact would you like it to have on other people?

Memorize

And Joshua set up at Gilgal the twelve stones they had taken out of the Jordan. He said to the Israelites, "In the future when your descendants ask their fathers, 'What do these stones mean?' tell them, 'Israel crossed the Jordan on dry ground.' For the LORD your God dried up the Jordan.... He did this so that all the peoples of the earth might know that the hand of the LORD is powerful and so that you might always fear the LORD your God."

Joshua 4:20–24

Day four/A place for every stone

The Very Words of God

God has arranged the parts in the body, every one of them, just as he wanted them to be.... Now you are the body of Christ, and each one of you is a part of it.

1 Corinthians 12:18, 27

Bible Discovery

Shaped for a Specific Purpose

Nothing is more lifeless than stone. Yet in the right hands and right circumstances, nothing is more useful, lasting, and beautiful. When God uses stones and rocks as his instruments, great miracles happen. One of those miracles is the way God is building the "living stones" of all believers into a magnificent temple that will display his honor and glory to the world.

God gives every believer—every living stone—a unique and important place in his temple. The temple wouldn't be complete without each and every stone being in its proper place. Because every believer is like a rough building stone freshly cut from the quarry, God must shape each one to fit perfectly into its designated spot in his magnificent temple.

1. In 1 Corinthians 12, the apostle Paul gives us a picture of the importance of each and every believer in the *body* of Christ, which is another common image the writers of the Scriptures used to refer to the whole community of people who follow Jesus. As you read these verses, think of what is being said in terms of the temple metaphor.

   a. Read verses 4–11. What are the different gifts God gives to members of his community, and in what ways would these gifts show the greatness of God to the world? What is common to all of these diverse gifts? (Hint: in terms of source and purpose.) What would be the effect on the entire community if someone's gift is not recognized or used (or if a stone is missing)?

   b. Read verses 12–27. Why do you think God has made so many different parts? Is any part of the body of Christ more important than another? Why or why not? What is the effect when one part of the body is honored, or when one part suffers? What message is communicated to the members of the body and to those who see it functioning when every part is recognized, respected, and cared for? How do you think the new believers in Corinth and other places felt when they read this? Why?

c. Think of a believer who is an acclaimed living stone in your community. Then think of a living stone who is little noticed. In God's eyes, is one person less important? More important? Does God put any less care into shaping people who are "hidden" and receive little notice?

d. Why is every stone in God's temple and every part of the body important, even those that are not visible? How should this fact affect how we treat other believers, especially those who are not attractive or otherwise are not appreciated in our culture?

e. Does your faith community have a place for every "living stone"? Why or why not?

2. As God, Jesus was the Rock and shaped the stones he would use. But as a human, Jesus also was "shaped" to fulfill his Father's purpose. Jesus learned, grew, and submitted as any other human would, and he did it perfectly. In what ways was Jesus "shaped" and by whom? (See Philippians 2:6–8; Luke 2:51–52; Matthew 26:36–39; John 15:15.)

3. Who shapes and fits us to be the living stones of God's temple? What are some of the ways by which we are shaped? (See Hebrews 3:4; Ephesians 2:21–22; Jeremiah 23:29.)

4. When believers in Priene learned that they each were a special living stone whom God was chiseling for a specific place in his temple, what do you think it meant to them?

5. How might your life be different if you remember, every day, that you are God's presence — a "living stone" in his "temple" — wherever you are, to whomever you are with?

A Lesson from Temple Stones

Despite the destruction of God's temple in Jerusalem by the Romans in AD 70 and the passage of nearly two thousand years, the southwest corner of the Temple Mount still reflects images of its former glory. The temple platform is more than twelve hundred feet long and seven hundred feet wide, and the supporting walls are believed to contain more than two million stones! These stones, many weighing more than twenty-five tons, were an architectural marvel in Jesus' day, as they are in ours. Each stone came from a quarry miles away, and skilled stone cutters precisely fit each stone into place without cement.

Archaeologists who dug beneath the street of Jesus' time found the foundation stones of these temple walls—stones that no one was ever supposed to see. The stones were as carefully chiseled and placed (and as beautiful) as the visible stones! The care and precision illustrated in the construction of the temple reminds us of the care Jesus takes in shaping us, as living stones, to fit perfectly into our designated place in the temple he is building.

Reflection

Why do you, and every other believer, need to be "shaped" by God?

In what way(s) has God "chipped" on you? Consider the pleasant as well as the unpleasant experiences God has used to shape you so you would fit into your rightful place in his "house."

In which area(s) might Jesus be carefully shaping you to be a living stone to fit into his "house," the temple of the Holy Spirit? What is he using in your life to shape you for his purposes? In what way(s) is his work making you a better stone?

For what purpose or place in God's temple do you believe God is shaping you? In what ways does the stone he wants you to be fit perfectly with the other stones in his "house"?

Did You Know?

The Bible records in Matthew 13:55 and Mark 6:3 that Jesus, like his father, Joseph, was a carpenter (*tekton*; Greek). *Tekton* refers to a builder. Since builders used stone in most construction in the New Testament world, it is probable that a *tekton* worked with stone as well as wood. Scholars believe that Jesus likely worked in an ancient quarry on a hilltop about two miles from Nazareth.

DAY FIVE/A COMMUNITY OF LOVE

The Very Words of God

"A new command I give you: Love one another. As I have loved you, so you must love one another. By this all men will know that you are my disciples, if you love one another."

John 13:34–35

Bible Discovery

Love Makes All the Difference

Christians today often emphasize correct doctrine or adherence to certain practices as the proof of our faith. These are essential, of course, but doctrine and ritual do not prove our faith to anyone. They do not make a suitable temple to display the greatness and goodness of God to the world. Jesus told his disciples what kind of temple the world would notice. Let's see what he taught and how his disciples responded.

1. How would people in cities like Priene know that the faith of the disciples of Jesus was genuine? (See John 13:34–35.)

2. What kinds of things destroy love in the body of Christ as well as its testimony? (See 1 Corinthians 3:3–4; 6:1–8.)

3. Read John 17:20–26.

   a. What was Jesus' prayer for his disciples? What did he want for them and why is it significant? What would the world know if believers lived this way?

   b. In what ways was this prayer answered in the lives of the early Christians?

   c. In what ways is it being answered in the lives of Christians today?

4. What in God's eyes is truly valuable in the community of faith? What does God command his community—his "temple"—to do and for what purpose? (See Galatians 5:6; 1 Peter 2:9–12.)

5. In the context of the passages you read for question 4, how does the tendency of many believers today to reduce faith to theology and the transfer of information affect unbelieving people around us?

6. Think about believers you know—at home, at church, at work, in your community. In what ways do you love each of them as a valuable member of the body of Christ and a "living stone" of God's house? In what ways might you be treating some people as more or less important than others?

Reflection

Read James 2:14–26 several times.

How much does the "temple" where God lives in your community provide for the needs of local people, as the temple of Athena did, and as Jesus commanded us to do?

To what extent are you and your faith community accomplishing the purposes intended for God's temple in your community? Where are you willing to make improvements? How willing are you to be "shaped" for God's purposes?

Memorize

But you are a chosen people, a royal priesthood, a holy nation, a people belonging to God, that you may declare the praises of him who called you out of darkness into his wonderful light.... Live such good lives among the pagans that, though they accuse you of doing wrong, they may see your good deeds and glorify God on the day he visits us.

1 Peter 2:9, 12

The very words of god

Jesus' disciples, like most of the Jewish people in Galilee, were deeply committed to learning, living, teaching, and praying the Hebrew Scriptures—the Word of the living God. They loved and memorized the Word. They recited it daily, individually and in synagogue communities. They listened to rabbis interpret and teach it. They debated how to understand it and live it. They passed it from generation to generation. Devotion to Scripture was the foundation of the disciples' faith, community, and message to others.

Above all, Jesus' disciples sought to obey the text as Jesus interpreted it, taught it, and demonstrated it every day of his life. Jesus' oral teaching passed from rabbi to disciple to disciple, just as Jews had done for a thousand years. Inspired writers such as Luke, John, Paul, James, and Peter quoted the Hebrew Bible or quoted Jesus quoting and interpreting it. They recognized that God had given them his Word and that he expected them to faithfully speak it to others. Speaking, teaching, and living the Word of God was (and still is) what makes disciples.

But how could the disciples make disciples among Hellenistic people who knew little, if anything, about the Word of God? Certainly the Greeks and Romans needed guidance on how to live, but unlike the Jews they had no sacred writings. They believed myriad versions of myths, which were not considered holy. Greek poets were often thought to be inspired by the muses, but this did not make their poetry the words of the gods. Pagan priests provided little help because they focused on the ceremony and ritual of public worship, which mostly had to do with offerings to please particular gods. The Greek and Roman culture of Asia Minor had no sense of the kind of divine revelation that Jesus' followers understood, so how would the disciples interest that world in the words of God?

Their lack of sacred texts did not mean the people of Asia Minor lacked interest in hearing from their gods, however. Modern archaeology indicates that they craved such information and expended great effort to seek divine revelations. In magnificent temples such as the temple of Apollo at Didyma, a seeker could bring a question and receive an "oracle," supposedly a divine revelation in the god's very words. That hunger for words from their gods gave Jesus' disciples significant opportunities to share the Word of the living God throughout Asia.

This session is set among the ruins of the magnificent temple of Apollo at Didyma, not far from Miletus where Paul visited. Didyma is not mentioned in the Bible, but it most certainly was known to Jesus' disciples in Asia Minor. It provides a stunning environment in which to consider the importance of the Word of God during ancient times and today. We'll explore our commitment to the Word of God and our opportunities to provide its blessing to people today.

opening Thoughts (3 minutes)

The Very Words of God

Josiah got rid of the mediums and spiritists, the household gods, the idols and all the other detestable things seen in Judah and Jerusalem. This he did to fulfill the requirements of the law .... Neither before nor after Josiah was there a king like him who turned to the LORD as he did—with all his heart and with all his soul and with all his strength, in accordance with all the Law of Moses.

2 Kings 23:24–25

Think About It

What does it mean to you to be able to pick up a Bible and actually read what God has said? If you didn't have a Bible, how would you know what God wanted you to know? Where would you go to find out what God had to say to you about your life?

DVD Notes (30 minutes)

Jesus and the text

The road to Didyma

The oracle of Apollo at Didyma

To receive an oracle

We have the very words of God!

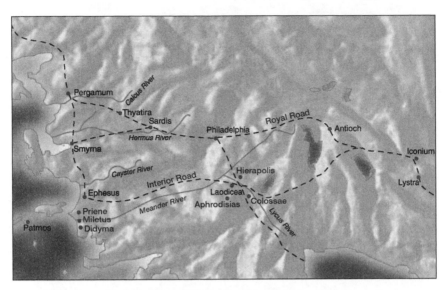

The oracle of Apollo at Didyma was located about twelve miles south of Miletus and about two miles from the sea.

DVD Highlights (4 minutes)

1. As you viewed the ruins of the great Apollo temple at Didyma, what were you thinking? What impressed you? What surprised you?

2. How would you describe what brought people to Didyma—for a thousand years? What was their need? What created their sense of wonder and awe when they heard the words they believed came from Apollo? What did an oracle from Apollo mean to them?

3. What challenge did Ray present at the end of this DVD segment? What did you realize today about the value of the holy Scriptures that hadn't impressed you before?

For Greater Understanding ...
What Is an Oracle?

Ancient people had a great need to hear a revelation—to receive an *oracle*—from their gods. An oracle is "information transmitted from the deity to human beings," that usually provides "answers to important questions or revelations about future events."[1] The word *oracle* has a number of meanings. It can refer to:

- the words believed to be received by the priestess from the god,
- the process of hearing that word,
- the medium or priestess who received the word from the god,
- the shrine or temple where people could come to seek an oracle,
- a divine revelation.

---

small Group Bible Discovery and Discussion (14 minutes)

God's Word on the Oracles

For people in the world of the Bible, seeking what was believed to be the word of a god—an oracle—was a familiar practice. Before the time of Abraham, the Egyptians had sought oracles. By the time of Jesus and his disciples, the Greeks and Romans had been seeking oracles for hundreds of years and had built elaborate temples where people came to receive an oracle.

During its history, Israel often was tempted to abandon obedience to God's Word and adopt the practices of their pagan neighbors. Seeking divine revelation from sources other than God—consulting oracles or mediums, or by divination—was one of those practices. Let's see how God viewed the pagan oracles.

1. What does God say about seeking divine revelation from pagan oracles or fortune telling, and how will he respond to those who seek such revelations? (See Leviticus 19:31; 20:6; Hosea 4:1, 12.)

2. Jeremiah 23:25–40 describes a type of false oracle.

   a. What is it about seeking oracles that so greatly offends God? (See verses 27–32, 36.)

   b. What will God do when prophets invent oracles but claim they are from the true God? (See verses 39–40.)

3. What was God's warning to his people regarding oracles and other pagan practices before they entered the land of Canaan? (See Deuteronomy 18:9–13.)

4. From that same Deuteronomy passage, what did God say would be the results of pagan oracles, such as the oracle of Apollo at Didyma, on his people?

How do these results differ from the impact the Word of God has on people?

5. In what ways do God's views about divination differ from popular views of divination today?

6. In what ways is the need of ancient people to hear an oracle from their gods similar to what people do today to satisfy their desire to be in communion with some kind of spiritual force or being? In what ways is it different?

What "speaks" to people today? Does anything like Didyma exist in our world?

What is the danger of seeking oracles from false gods and spirits?

ꜰaith Lesson (3 minutes)

Read 2 Kings 23:24–25 and consider whether or not it is possible to be a disciple of Jesus—to follow the Rabbi with all your heart, soul, and strength—and dabble in revelations from any source other than God.

1. What "wisdom" are you tempted to seek that doesn't come from God? In what ways does that wisdom hinder you from following the Rabbi with your whole being?

2. How diligently do you seek the wisdom of God as revealed in the Scriptures? How much effort are you willing to put into seeking God's wisdom—reading, studying, and memorizing the text—in order to learn to walk as Jesus walked?

closing (1 minute)

Read the following verse aloud. Then pray, asking God to help you be faithful in hiding his Word in your heart and learning to walk as Jesus walked.

Memorize

I have hidden your word in my heart that I might not sin against you.
Psalm 119:11

walking with the rabbi day by day
In-Depth Personal Study Sessions

Day one/In awe of the oracles

The Very Words of God

Seek the LORD while he may be found; call on him while he is near.

Isaiah 55:6

Bible Discovery

Hungry for a Word from God

Ancient Eastern people—Gentiles as well as Jews—placed great value on divine revelation. To their way of thinking, a "word" was more than sound, it was a living thing that performed an action. Thus the words they received from a divine being were living words that would accomplish what they expressed. No wonder the Jews were in awe of God's words! No wonder the Gentiles took the oracle of Apollo very seriously!

The effort ancient Gentiles expended to construct the road to Didyma and to build a temple of the magnitude of the Apollo temple shows how greatly they esteemed the oracles of Apollo. Their personal commitment to travel great distances to receive an oracle highlight how desperate they were for a word of divine advice, warning, or encouragement. The following passages of Scripture will help you see the awe and respect the Jewish people had for the Word of God.

1. How does the psalmist view God's Word? What is his response to God's laws? (See Psalm 119:114–116, 120.)

2. According to Isaiah 66:5, how did God's people respond when they read or heard God's Word recited?

3. When God came down to speak his words to Moses, what happened that filled the people with awe? How did the people respond? (See Exodus 19:9, 16–19.)

4. Remember, in the minds of ancient people, words and actions were inseparable. They expected the divine word to accomplish something. Read Genesis 1:11–12; Psalm 107:19–22; Isaiah 55:10–11.

   a. Note in each case what God's Word accomplishes.

   b. In what ways do you think what God's Word accomplishes helps people recognize his presence and his power?

5. Given your understanding of the importance of God's Word, read John 1:1–3, 14–18.

   a. How do you think Jews would have responded to John's description of Jesus as the "Word"? In what ways does this differ from the way we would respond?

   b. What might they have thought about Jesus' words and his actions?

6. Read the Data File on the Apollo temple at Didyma that begins below. How highly valued was divine revelation in that culture?

Data File

In Awe of the Oracle

For nearly a thousand years, people traveled to Didyma to seek the oracles of Apollo. The Greeks built the first temple at the shrine of Apollo at Didyma in the eighth century BC. In 494 BC the Persians destroyed the temple, but in 334 BC Alexander the Great initiated its rebuilding over the ruins of the previous temple. Finishing touches were still being put on the massive temple in AD 37–41 during the reign of Caligula.

The sacred road from Miletus to Didyma

It's important to realize that Didyma was never a city; it was always a shrine. The nearest city was Miletus, about fifteen miles away. Devotees of Apollo traveled a paved road that began at the shrine of Apollo in Miletus, wound its way to a small seaport on the Aegean Sea, and ended near the entrance of the sacred area of the temple of Apollo at Didyma. No expense was spared in building such an important road. The curbed road has paving stones six to eight inches thick, and in some places a sewer channel runs beneath it. The entire length of the road was lined with shops for celebrants of the Apollo festivals and inquirers of the oracle. The final stretch of road was lined with statues representing priests, priestesses, and reclining lions. As a person approached Didyma on the sacred road, there could be no doubt that something of great importance lay just ahead.

The Apollo temple at Didyma. Each of its 124 columns was more than six feet in diameter and more than sixty-two feet tall.

The temple itself would take your breath away. It was the second largest temple built in the ancient world. The peak of the roof stood nearly 100 feet high. The temple building was surrounded by a raised platform that measured 390 feet east to west and 190 feet wide! On that platform, in dipteral style (two rows), stood 124 columns that supported the massive roof structure of the Apollo temple. Each fluted column was more than six feet in diameter and more than sixty-two feet tall. It took a lifetime of labor (fifty-five years) to make just one column! Imagine how impressive your first glimpse of that temple would have been! The Apollo temple would have been unlike anything you had ever seen before. Imagine how important the oracle was to these people.

As petitioners approached the doorway to the oracle chamber, their awe for the god Apollo would only have intensified. They climbed broad stairs up to the temple platform and stood in the *pronaos* (the forecourt) amidst what must have seemed like a forest of massive columns. Before them was the doorway to the oracle chamber where the priest would hear their request and eventually deliver the oracle. The opening was forty-five feet tall and eighteen feet wide! The one-piece marble door posts stood forty-five feet tall and weighed about eighty tons each!

The *pronaos* of the Apollo temple at Didyma, where petitioners would wait for an oracle. The raised area in the background is the doorway where the priest would stand to speak.

The doors to the oracle chamber would remain closed until the priest was ready to speak. Then, with great drama, the massive doors would swing open. The people would stand and look up to the priest, who stood in the doorway several feet above them. The priest would hear petitions for the oracle and would deliver the oracle in verse. Then the doors would close again. Sometimes people waited for months before their oracle was given. Imagine the awe a person must have felt when he finally received a word from the god Apollo.

Did You Know?

Seeking divine revelation was important to the Gentiles of the ancient world. They sought oracles in many ways—by throwing dice, analyzing flocks of birds or animal livers, interpreting dreams or the movements of the planets. At shrines such as the oracle of Apollo at Didyma, people would line up to seek a word from a god given through a priest or priestess. Usually only those of higher economic status received a word from the gods. They could afford the required sacrifices and gifts to the god. Poor people could only look on as spectators because the gods favored the rich and powerful.

Reflection

In what way(s) have these passages from Scripture and descriptions of the Apollo oracle helped you to understand the deep awe and respect ancient people had for divine revelation?

Why do you think they had such a hunger to hear from god? What about you? How deep is your hunger to hear from God? What are you willing to do to satisfy that hunger?

Because hearing God's Word or reciting it yourself is to experience God, what happens when a believer in Jesus has little knowledge of or exposure to the Word of God?

Based on what you've discovered today, how can you begin to experience more of God's power and presence in your life? What fills you with awe for God's Word?

Memorize

Ask and it will be given to you; seek and you will find; knock and the door will be opened to you. For everyone who asks receives; he who seeks finds; and to him who knocks, the door will be opened.

Matthew 7:7–8

Imagine ...
To Receive an Oracle

Although we don't know the exact practices of the Apollo oracle at Didyma, we do have a general idea of how it operated from what we know about other oracles (Cuma in Italy, Delphi in Greece, and Klaros in Asia). The practices weren't exactly the same, but they were at least similar. So imagine for a moment that you are a member of a family seeking a revelation from Apollo. As you read through the process, try to imagine yourself doing these things in hopes of receiving an oracle. Think about how important the oracle was to you, how much you were willing to do and sacrifice in the hope of receiving a word from the great Apollo.

- Prepare for the experience while traveling on the sacred road to Didyma.
- Wash at the sacred well.
- Wash a sacrificial sheep or goat at the well.
- Make a sacrifice at which time a priest determined (based on the animal's behavior or liver, for example) whether Apollo was willing to hear your petition.
- Wait in the pronaos for the door to open so the priest could hear the request.
- Ask the question, which the priest of Apollo heard.
- Wait (possibly for months) while the priest gave the question to Pythia, the priestess who went into a trance to "hear" from Apollo.
- Wait longer while the priests put her uttering into verse.
- Watch the door of the *chresmographeion* (a building located immediately adjacent to the pronaos, the oracle office) open and listen intently as the verse, which you believe are the very words of the god Apollo, are recited to you.
- Leave a gift to thank Apollo for his revelation because his answer depended on his continued good favor.

Day Two/The Oracles of the Living God!

The Very Words of God

O my people, hear my teaching; listen to the words of my mouth.

Psalm 78:1

Bible Discovery

The Bible Is God's Oracle

Initially, the word *oracle* in the Hebrew Bible referred to parts of the text that were pronouncements from God through his messengers (usually prophets) given in response to specific inquiries. Over time, *oracle* became another word for the entire Bible. Thus the Bible is an oracle comprised of all God's words that have been pronounced, either directly or through an inspired messenger's writing, in response to human questions. As you explore some of the Bible passages that deal with oracles, consider how God speaks not only in response to the questions of his people, but in a way that makes him known to those who would acknowledge him, acclaim him, and obey him.

1. From the time the Israelites left Egypt, the Hebrew Scriptures record a history of oracles, a sampling of which are listed below. Consider each of the following examples and note who is giving the oracle, the ultimate source of the oracle, and why it is being given.

   a. Numbers 23:5–12, 16–18 (for the complete story, read Numbers 22:1–24:25)

   b. Psalm 36:1–4

   c. Isaiah 13:1–22 (the first of a series of oracles continuing with Isaiah 14:28; 15:1; 17:1; 19:1; 21:1, 11, 13; 22:1; 23:1)

   d. Ezekiel 12:8–16

e. Nahum 1:1 – 14

2. Often God gave an oracle in response to specific questions asked
    by his people. Read each of the following and note the question
    asked and God's response:

Scripture	Question(s) Asked	God's Answer(s)
2 Samuel 5:18–25		
2 Chronicles 20:1 – 18		
Habakkuk 1:1 – 11		
Malachi 1:1 – 5		

3. What recurring themes do you see in these passages that relate
    to what we have been studying about walking in the footsteps of
    the Rabbi? What do you think might be God's purpose in giving
    oracles?

Profile of Oracles

The Oracles of Apollo	The Oracles of the Living God
Available only to those who can afford them	Available to everyone who seeks them
The wealthy and powerful received first priority	All people are equal before him
Signs indicated if an answer would be given	Will answer all who seek him
Priestess (high on some substance) is needed to convey the message	Communicates directly to everyone through his Word
Requires elaborate ceremony and building(s)	Can speak anywhere his Word is found
Gave small revelations	In Scripture we have in our possession the entire oracle of God

Reflection

The Greeks and Romans who sought an oracle from Apollo could only hope that the sacrifice and gifts they offered would earn the god's consideration of their request. In contrast, God welcomes all who seek him. Read each of the following passages and ask yourself, *What does God desire for his people? What does he promise to those who seek him?*

Deuteronomy 4:29 – 31

1 Chronicles 16:10 – 11

Psalm 9:10

Jeremiah 29:12 – 13

Zechariah 8:21 – 22

Matthew 7:7 – 8

Then ask, *How badly do I want to know what God says? Do I truly believe that he wants me to seek him? What is my commitment to seek him in his oracles—the inspired words of Scripture?*

Memorize

Seek the LORD *while he may be found; call on him while he is near.*

Isaiah 55:6

DAY THREE/JESUS LIVED THE TEXT

The Very Words of God

And we have the word of the prophets made more certain, and you will do well to pay attention to it, as to a light shining in a dark place.... Above all, you must understand that no prophecy of Scripture came about by the prophet's own interpretation. For prophecy never had its origin in the will of man, but men spoke from God as they were carried along by the Holy Spirit.

2 Peter 1:19–21

Bible Discovery

Walking by the Eternal Word (Oracle) of God

Jesus and his disciples, and later their disciples, highly valued the oracles, the very Word of God. They were committed to learning, living, teaching, praying, and even dying with the holy Scriptures on their lips. They memorized the text, quoted it, and thanked God for it. In contrast, many Christians today spend little time reading, studying, and memorizing Scripture. Instead of walking as Jesus walked, we tend to walk our own paths as if the Scripture is a distant memory. Take a closer look at how essential the Word of God was to every step Jesus took.

1. Read Matthew 26:31; Mark 7:5–8; 14:27; Luke 18:31–33; 21:20–22; 24:44–48; and John 8:17–18; 10:33–36 and take note of Jesus' knowledge and use of Scripture. Note particularly how essential the text was to his everyday life and how easily the oracles of God recorded in the Hebrew Bible flowed from him in his everyday conversations.

    a. How essential was Jesus' knowledge of God's Word to his everyday life?

    b. Based on Jesus' example in these passages, how important ought the living Word of God to be in the daily lives of his disciples who seek to walk as he walked?

Did You Know?

In the book of Matthew alone, Jesus is recorded quoting from the Hebrew Bible at least thirty-eight times!

---

2. Read Matthew 11:7–15 and notice the evidence Jesus used to show that John the Baptist was the forerunner of the Messiah. Considering how highly the Jews valued the Word of God, what impact would his knowledge and quotation of the Hebrew have made on his listeners? Do you think Jesus would have had a greater or lesser impact if he had used his own words? Why or why not?

3. When Jesus quoted from the Scriptures in John 7:37–43, did his listeners take his words seriously? What does their struggle to interpret his meaning indicate about the importance of what he said? In what ways do you think their response would have been different if Jesus had said the same thing without referring to the Scriptures?

4. According to Luke 24:13–27, two of the disciples struggled to comprehend what Jesus' death and resurrection meant. Imagine what it must have been like for them to hear Jesus explain everything that the Word of God had said about him. How much awe would you have felt as the events you had witnessed and the spoken Word of God suddenly made sense? How might you have felt the presence of God in those events and with you? In what ways would the Word of God have encouraged and strengthened you to walk as Jesus walked?

Reflection

Read Matthew 4:2 – 10. Notice how easily Jesus uses the Word of God. Notice how powerful the Word of God is and what it accomplishes.

> How did Jesus know these passages from the Hebrew Bible? What does his knowledge and use of Scripture tell you about how important God's Word was to him?

> To what extent are you able to connect Scripture texts to the thoughts and conversations of your daily life? Why is it important to be able to do this?

> As you consider your walk through life, how seriously do you take Scripture — the complete oracle of the living God? What step will you take to make God's living Word a more essential part of your daily life?

Memorize

Whoever claims to live [Greek: walk] in him must walk as Jesus did.
1 John 2:6

Day four/Remembering the word of god

The Very Words of God

For you have been born again, not of perishable seed, but of imperishable, through the living and enduring word of God.

1 Peter 1:23

Bible Discovery

Jesus' Disciples Knew the Scriptures

Because Jesus was deeply committed to the Scripture, we would expect his disciples to be as well, and they were. The disciples of Jesus participated in God's great act of redemption and could recall those events personally. They also had obeyed God's command to remember his Word by memorizing large portions of the Hebrew Bible. Their knowledge of the text and their passion for it gave them the confidence and power to take the life-changing message of the kingdom of God to the world. As you study their spontaneous use of Scripture, take note of their attitude toward the very words of God. Notice how thoroughly they knew the Scriptures and how deeply committed they were to be like Jesus.

Did You Know?

Peter, and the other "inner circle" disciples, had an extensive knowledge of Scripture. Like their Rabbi, they lived by the Word of God and used it in their teaching and everyday conversations. Consider, for a moment, Peter's use of the Old Testament in his first letter.

- 1 Peter 1:16 quotes Leviticus 11:44 – 45; 19:2.
- 1 Peter 1:24 – 25 quotes Isaiah 40:6 – 8.
- 1 Peter 2:6 quotes Isaiah 28:16.

- 1 Peter 2:7 quotes Psalm 118:22.
- 1 Peter 2:8 quotes Isaiah 8:14.
- 1 Peter 2:9–10 hints at the exodus of Israel and echoes Exodus 19:5–6.
- 1 Peter 2:22 quotes Isaiah 53:9.
- 1 Peter 2:24–25 quotes Isaiah 53:4–6.
- 1 Peter 3:6 refers to Abraham and Sarah.
- 1 Peter 3:10–12 quotes Psalm 34:12–16.
- 1 Peter 3:14 quotes Isaiah 8:12.
- 1 Peter 3:20–21 refers to Noah.
- 1 Peter 4:18 quotes Proverbs 11:31.
- 1 Peter 5:5 quotes Proverbs 3:34.

Think About It!

Can you imagine knowing and referring to as much Scripture as Peter does?

What feelings do these references to God's oracles, given long before Peter wrote, stir up in your soul? Would Peter's words be as meaningful to you if he had not quoted the oracles?

In what ways does Peter's example inspire you to value God's Word?

1. What equipped John the Baptist to answer the questions of the priests and Levites? (See John 1:19–27.) As you read this passage, take note of the interaction between people who knew the text!

2. What formed the basis of the disciples' prayer recorded in Acts 4:23–26? What do you think they thought and felt as they prayed the very words of King David that spoke to their situation?

3. Stephen was on trial before the Sanhedrin because those who wanted to argue against him "could not stand up against his wisdom or the Spirit by whom he spoke" (Acts 6:10).

   a. Stephen's stirring defense is recorded in Acts 7:1–50. Take the time to read this passage and imagine how his Jewish audience received it. How do you think they felt as he recounted the oracles of God and their fulfillment in history?

   b. In what way do you think Stephen's recitation of Jewish history and the very words of God influenced what happened next? Why? (See Acts 7:51–58.)

4. Read Acts 8:26–39. What enabled Philip to provide an explanation of the Scriptures to the Ethiopian eunuch? What effect did recounting the Word of God and its fulfillment have? Is this what you would expect? Why?

5. What did Paul do in Antioch, and how was he able to do this? (See Acts 13:13–43.) What effect did recounting the Word of God and its fulfillment have? Is this what you would expect? Why?

6. The disciples of Jesus not only relied on the Word of God to make new disciples, they relied on the Hebrew Scriptures in order to understand what Jesus did while he was with them. Read each of the following passages and note what the disciples' knowledge of God's Word helped them understand.

What the Disciples Witnessed	What They Remembered	What They Understood
John 2:12–17		
John 2:18–22		
John 12:12–16		

Reflection

Before Israel ever entered the Promised Land, God knew that they would want a king to rule over them. So in Deuteronomy 17:18–20, God told Moses how the king was to view the words of God. Read God's instructions carefully and record what God commanded the king to do and why it was so important.

Why are the oracles of the living God essential in the life of everyone who follows him? Are they any less important to the king of Israel, to Jesus' disciples, to you?

Are you immersed enough in God's Word for it to influence your thoughts and everyday speech as was true for Jesus' disciples? Why or why not?

How might your life be different if you viewed God's Word as highly as the early disciples did?

Memorize

> *It [the word of God] is to be with him, and he is to read it all the days of his life so that he may learn to revere the* LORD *his God and follow carefully all the words of this law and these decrees.*
>
> Deuteronomy 17:19

Day Five/Becoming a Man or Woman of the Text

The Very Words of God

> *I have chosen the way of truth; I have set my heart on your laws. I hold fast to your statutes, O* LORD.
>
> Psalm 119:30–31

Bible Discovery

Treasure the Words of God

Jesus came from a community that highly valued and knew the Scriptures, and he did as well. He expected his disciples to follow his example and become like him, and he expects no less from his followers today. Yet many Christians today do not know much about the text he knew and loved—the Bible—and have memorized little or none of it. How can we possibly do what Jesus commands if we do not know his Word? When Bible literacy is at an all-time low in Western culture, we must commit ourselves to remember the Word of God so that we will be equipped, as were Jesus' disciples, to go into the world and make disciples. We must treasure and learn the Word of God so that we can in turn speak the "very words" (oracles) of God.

1. Every great follower of God who is remembered today knew and treasured the Word of God. You have examined the attitudes of Jesus and his disciples toward God's Word. Now take a look at some of the great followers of God who lived before Jesus. What did each of them express about their view of God's Word?

    a. Moses in Deuteronomy 8:1–5

    b. Job in Job 23:10–12

    c. David in Psalm 119:97–104

    d. Jeremiah in Jeremiah 15:16

    e. Ezekiel in Ezekiel 2:8–3:4; 3:10–11

2. In what ways does the perspective of these faithful servants of God deepen your appreciation for the Word of God that has been handed down to you? What action does their love for God's Word prompt you to take regarding your own relationship with God's Word?

3. How do the attitudes of Jesus, the great leaders of Israel, and the early disciples toward the Word of God differ from the attitudes of popular culture? Of Christians in general? Of your faith community?

Think About It

To an ancient Jewish believer, the *word* (oracle) was an act of God's power that accomplished what it said. God makes things happen simply by speaking his word. Reading God's inspired Word, by the power of the Word and the Holy Spirit accompanying it, will produce within the reader the desires it demands. If you seek a commitment to more greatly desire God and his Word, then be in the Word. Reading the Word will create a greater desire for the Word!

4. What do you think Christians today can do to reclaim the hunger for and commitment to God's sacred Word?

5. What is God revealing to you about your commitment to his Word? How dedicated are you to knowing your Bible and using it as the foundation for your witness and life? What challenges must you overcome in order to become a student of God's Word — reading, studying, praying his eternal "oracle"?

6. God instructed his people to do certain things to keep his words and commands foremost in their minds. What did he tell them to do? What everyday practices would accomplish the same thing in your life? What tangible reminders of God and his words would be meaningful to you? (See Numbers 15:37–41; Deuteronomy 6:4–9.)

Reflection

Psalm 119:89–94, 145–152 are just a few of many verses that express the psalmist's deep, abiding attitude toward the Word of God. Read these verses and consider all that the words of God mean to you — how God wants to share his Word with anyone who asks him; how powerful and life-giving God's Word is; how essential it is to know it; how necessary it is to obey it; what a gift it is to share God's Word with others who are hungry to hear it. Then write a psalm from the depths of your heart that expresses your relationship with God's Word.

Did You Know?

It is said that a rabbi and his disciples who desire to be like him must:

- Learn the text.
- Live the text.
- Teach the text.
- Pray the text.
- Die the text.

Memorize

Each one should use whatever gift he has received to serve others, faithfully administering God's grace in its various forms. If anyone speaks, he should do it as one speaking the very words of God.

1 Peter 4:10–11

notes

Session 1: When the Rabbi Says "Come"

1. Dallas Willard, *The Spirit of the Disciplines* (San Francisco: Harper-SanFrancisco, 1990), 259–260.
2. The Mishnah contains rabbinic interpretations of Scripture written down during the second century AD. Jewish scholars believe it contains the oral traditions present during the first century BC to first century AD, and therefore would reflect what was true during Jesus' lifetime.

Session 5: The Very Words of God

1. "Oracle," Frank T. Miosi, in *Anchor Bible Dictionary*, vol. 5, ed. David Noel Freedman (New York: Doubleday, 1992).

Bibliography

Books

Akurgal, Ekrem. *Ancient Civilizations and Ruins of Turkey*, 9th ed. Izmir: Net Turistik, 2001.

Arav, Rami, and Richard A. Freund. *Bethsaida*, 2 vols. Kirksville, Mo.: Thomas Jefferson University Press, 1999.

Aune, D. E. *Prophecy in Early Christianity and the Ancient Mediterranean World*. Grand Rapids, Mich.: Eerdmans, 1983 (pp. 23–79).

Banks, Robert. *Going to Church in the First Century*. Jacksonville, Fla.: Christian Books, 1990.

Beitzel, Barry J. *Moody Bible Atlas of Bible Lands*. Chicago: Moody Press, 1993.

Bivin, David. *Understanding the Difficult Words of Jesus*. Shippensburg, Pa.: Destiny Image, 1994.

Bonhoeffer, Dietrich. *The Cost of Discipleship*, New York: MacMillan, 1959.

De Boer, J. Z., J. R. Hale, and J. Chanton. "New Evidence for the Geological Origins of the Ancient Dephic Oracle (Greece)." *Geology* 2001.

De Boer, Jelle Z. and John R. Hale. "Was She Really Stoned? The Oracle of Delphi." *Odyssey*, November–December 2002, vol. 5, no. 6.

DeVries, LaMoine F. *Cities of the Biblical World*. Peabody, Mass.: Hendrickson, 1997.

Edmonds, Anna G. *Turkey's Religious Sites*. Istanbul: Damko, 1997.

Fant, Clyde E., and Mitchell G. Reddish. *A Guide to Biblical Sites in Greece and Turkey*. London: Oxford University Press, 2003.

Farnell, L. *The Cults of the Greek City States*, vol. 4. Oxford, 1907 (pp. 98–355).

Finnegan, Jack. *Myth and Mystery: An Introduction to the Pagan Religions of the Biblical World*. Grand Rapids, Mich.: Baker, 1989.

Fitzmyer, Joseph A. *The Acts of the Apostles*. The Anchor Bible Commentary Series. New York: Doubleday, 1997.

Flusser, David. *Jesus*. Jerusalem: Magnes Press, 1997.

Fontenrose, J. *The Delphic Oracle*. Berkeley, Calif.: University of California Press, 1978.

Gehring, Roger. *House Church and Mission*. Peabody, Mass.: Hendrickson, 2004.

Gill, David, and Conrad Gempf. *The Book of Acts in Its Greco-Roman Setting* (vol. 2 of 6-vol. series, The Book of Acts in Its First-Century Setting). Grand Rapids, Mich.: Eerdmans, 1994.

Gradel, Ittai. *Emperor Worship and Roman Religion*. London: Oxford University Press, 2004.

Jeffers, James S. *The Greco-Roman World of the New Testament Era*. Downers Grove, Ill.: InterVarsity Press, 1999.

Kraybill, J. Nelson. *Imperial Cult and Commerce in John's Apocalypse*. Sheffield, Eng.: Academic Press, 1996.

Lachs, Samuel Tobias. *A Rabbinic Commentary on the New Testament*. Hoboken, N.J.: Ktav, 1987.

Levinskaya, Irina. *The Book of Acts in Its Diaspora Setting* (vol. 5 of 6-vol. series, The Book of Acts in Its First-Century Setting). Grand Rapids, Mich.: Eerdmans, 1994.

Meeks, Wayne. *The First Urban Christians: The Social World of the Apostle Paul*. New Haven, Conn.: Yale University Press, 1982.

Nun, Mendel. "Ancient Stone Anchors and Net Sinkers from the Sea of Galilee," in *The Sea of Galilee and Its Fishermen*. En Gev: Kibbutz En Gev, 1992.

Osiek, Carolyn. *What Are They Saying about the Social Setting of the New Testament?* New York: Paulist Press, 1984.

Parke, H. W., and D. E. W. Wormell. *The Delphic Oracle, v. II: The Oracular Responses*, Blackwell, Eng.: Oxford, 1956.

Pixner, Bargil. *The Fifth Gospel: With Jesus Through Galilee*. Rosh Pina, Israel: Corazin Publishing, 1992.

Rousseau, John J., and Rami Arav. *Jesus and His World*. Minneapolis: Fortress Press, 1995.

Rumscheid, Frank. *Priene: A Guide to the Pompei of Asia Minor*. Turkey: Ege Yayinlari, 1998.

Safrai, Shmuel, M. Stern, D. Flusser, and W. C. Van Unnik. *The Jewish People in the First Century*, 9 vols. Amsterdam: Van Gorcum, 1974.

Saldarini, Anthony J. *Pharisees, Scribes and Sadducees in Palestinian Society*. Grand Rapids, Mich.: Eerdmans, 1988.

Stauffer, Ethelbert. *Christ and the Caesars*. Philadelphia: Westminster Press, 1955.

Stern, David H. *Jewish New Testament Commentary*. Clarksville, Md.: Jewish New Testament Publications, 1992.

Van't Veer, M. B. *My God Is Yahweh*. St. Catherines, Ont.: Paideia Press, 1980.

Visalli, Gayla. *After Jesus: The Triumph of Christianity*. New York: Reader's Digest, 1992.

Ward, Kaari. *Jesus and His Times*. New York: Reader's Digest, 1987.

White, L. Michael. *Building God's House in the Roman World*. Baltimore: Johns Hopkins University Press, 1990.

————. *The Social Origins of Christian Architecture*. Valley Forge, Pa.: Trinity Press International, Harvard Theological Studies, 1990.

Wilson, Marvin. *Our Father Abraham: Jewish Roots of the Christian Faith*. Grand Rapids, Mich.: Eerdmans, 1993.

Witherington III, Ben. *Conflict and Community in Corinth*. Grand Rapids, Mich.: Eerdmans, 1994.

Winter, Bruce W., and Andrew D. Clarke. *Ancient Literary Setting* (vol. 1 of 6-vol. series, The Book of Acts in Its First-Century Setting). Grand Rapids, Mich.: Eerdmans, 1994.

Wright, N. T. "Upstaging the Emperor." *Bible Review*, February 1998.

Yamauchi, Edwin. *The Archaelogy of New Testament Cities in Western Asia Minor*. Grand Rapids, Mich.: Baker, 1980.

Young, Brad. *Jesus the Jewish Theologian*. Peabody, Mass.: Hendrickson, 1995.

————. *The Jewish Background to the Lord's Prayer*. Austin, Tex.: Center for Judaic-Christian Studies, 1984.

Websites

www.ancientsandals.com/index.htm, 2005, Walking in Their Sandals.

www.bib-arch.org/, 2005, Biblical Archaeology (Illuminating Archaeology and the Bible).

www.bibleplaces.com/, 2005, Bible Places.com.

www.bibleplaces.com/bethsaida.htm, 2005, Bible Places.com.

www.bibleplaces.com/didyma.htm, 2005, Bible Places.com.

www.bluethread.com/glossary.htm, 2005, Bluethread Glossary.

www.bridgesforpeace.com/, 2005, Bridges for Peace; Your Israel Connection.

www.ctsp.co.il/LBS%20pages/LBS_beth_shean.htm, 2005, Christian Travel Study
    Programs, Ltd.

www.en-gedi.org/, 2005, En-Gedi Resource Center.

www.ffoz.org, 2005, First Fruits of Zion.

www.focusmm.com/acmil_mn.htm, 2005, Focus Multimedia Online Magazine.

www.focusmm.com/acpriene.htm, 2005, Focus on the World.

www.geocities.com/miletmuseum/didyma.htm, 2005, Yahoo!GeoCities: Didyma.

www.geocities.com/miletmuseum/priene.htm, 2005, Yahoo!GeoCities: Priene.

www.goddess-athena.org/Museum/Temples/Priene, 2005, The Museum of the
    Goddess Athena.

www.hebrew4christians.com/, 2005, Hebrew for Christians.

www.hebrew-streams.org/, 2005, Hebrew Streams (ancient Hebrew elements
    in the New Testament).

www.hebroots.org, 2005, Hebraic Roots of Christianity Global Network.

www.historylearningsite.co.uk/a_history_of_ancient_rome.htm.

www.jcstudies.com/, 2005, Dwight A. Pryor (a teaching ministry of the Center
    for Judaic-Christian Studies).

www.jerusalemperspective.com/, 2005, Jerusalem Perspective Online: Explor-
    ing the Jewish Background to the Life and Words of Jesus.

www.jewishencyclopedia.com/index.jsp, 2005, Jewish Encyclopedia.com.

www.jewishvirtuallibrary.org/jsource/Archaeology/archtoc.html, 2005, The
    Jewish Virtual Library.

www.js.org/, 2005, Jerusalem School of Synoptic Research.

www.learn.jts.edu/contents/, 2005, Jewish Theological Seminary of America.

www.macalester.edu/classics/omrit, 2005, Macalester Classics.

www.news.nationalgeographic.com/news/2001/08/0814_delphioracle.html,
    2005, National Geographic.

www.perseus.tufts.edu/cgi-bin/siteindex?entry=Didyma, 2005, Tufts Univer-
    sity Perseus Project.

www.perseus.tufts.edu/cgi-bin/siteindex?lookup=Priene, 2005, Tufts Univer-
    sity Perseus Digital Library.

www.philologos.org/__eb-lotj/default.htm, 2005, The Legends of the Jews.

www.pohick.org/sts/faqs.html, 2005, Synagogue Facts.

www.preservingbibletimes.org/, 2005, Preserving Bible Times: Because Context Matters.

www.princeton.edu/%7Epressman/jewish.html, 2005, Princeton University Library: Jewish Studies Resources.

www.religion.rutgers.edu/iho/index.html, 2005, Department of Religion at Rutgers University.

www.sacredsites.com/middle_east/turkey/didyma.htm, 2005, Places of Peace and Power: Sacred Sites and Pilgrimage Traditions of the World.

www.unc.edu/courses/rometech/public/content/transport/Adam_Pawluk/Contruction_and_Makeup_of_htm., 2005, The Construction and Makeup of Ancient Roman Roads by Adam Pawluk.

photo/map credits

Map, page 95: *NIV Study Bible*, © Zondervan, 2000
Illustration, page 121: Carolyn Stitch, Holland, MI
Photo, page 122: Gary Layda, Photographic Services, Nashville, TN
All other photos: Courtesy of Ray Vander Laan
All other maps: Courtesy of The Image Group

We want to hear from you. Please send your comments about this book to us in care of zreview@zondervan.com. Thank you.

ZONDERVAN.com/
AUTHORTRACKER
follow your favorite authors